SIMPLY

THE BEST...

RECIPES BY DESIGN

Designed, Edited, and
Manufactured by
Favorite Recipes® Press
an imprint of

FRP™

P.O. Box 305142
Nashville, Tennessee 37230
1-800-358-0560

Book design by Lynette Sesler

Art Direction by Steve Newman

Photos provided by Balthazar Korab

Original Columbus skyline design by
Jim Ponsford, art teacher at Central
Middle School, Columbus, Indiana

Artwork for design provided by
Winters Associates, Inc.

The Columbus skyline design
consists of North Christian Church,
First Baptist Church,
Cleo Rogers Memorial Library,
St. Peter's Lutheran Church,
Ameritech Switching Station Tubes,
First Christian Church,
Henry Moore's "Large Arch"
sculpture and Bartholomew
County Courthouse.

Library of Congress Number:
97-61505
ISBN: 0-9659299-0-6

Manufactured in the
United States of America
First Printing: 1997
7,500 copies

ACKNOWLEDGEMENTS

SIMPLY THE BEST...RECIPES BY DESIGN is a collection of community award-winning and all-time family favorite recipes from the residents of Columbus and Bartholomew County, Indiana. These recipes have been handed down from generation to generation, passed around among family members, and shared by friends and neighbors. We feel these recipes are Simply the Best.

We hope you enjoy these recipes as much as we enjoy preparing and serving them for our families and friends.

We regret that, due to the tremendous response to our request for recipes, we were unable to publish all of them in this edition.

COOKBOOK COMMITTEE

JACQUE CHAMBERS

MARY LU FOUTS

BETSY HELLER

JILL INGERSOLL

ANN KNOBLOCH

EVAN KNOX

MARION MARSHALL

XENIA MILLER

JEANNETTE NOLAN-WESTLAKE

JOYCE ORWIN

JOANNE SEITZ

COLUMBUS AREA VISITORS CENTER

LOCATED AT the corner of Fifth and Franklin streets, the Visitors Center is more than a place to gather information—it's a destination that can keep visitors entertained with its video presentations, state-of-the-art exhibits, and artistic displays. For a thorough introduction to the city, see the exhibit titled "Columbus, Indiana: People and Their Buildings," an overview of the community and its architectural development. The 15-minute laser disc presentation tells of the background and heritage of Columbus architecture.

Daily architectural tours led by volunteer guides allow visitors to explore first-hand our architectural treasures. Self-guided tour maps are also available. Custom tours for groups can be arranged.

"Yellow Neon Chandelier and Persian Window" is a striking piece that serves as a focal point in the Visitors Center two-story bay window and stairway. Done by world-renowned glass designer Dale Chihuly, this work of art consists of 900 pieces of hand-blown yellow glass.

The Gift Shop offers visitors a "bit of Columbus" to take home with them. Gifts for all occasions and unique souvenirs include handmade pottery, architectural and children's books, jewelry, glass, T-shirts, sweatshirts, and many more interesting items.

Call or write for a free Visitors Guide to unlock the treasures of Columbus:

Visitors Center
506 Fifth Street
Columbus, IN 47201

800-468-6564
812-378-2622
e-mail: visitcol@hsonline.net

Visit Columbus on-line:
http://www.columbus.in.us

CONTENTS

COLUMBUS AREA VISITORS CENTER

INTRODUCTION

COLUMBUS, INDIANA, founded in 1821, is a small midwestern city of 35,000 people. It is not unlike many others cities, but perhaps a little more convinced that it can solve its problems and a little more possessed of a determination to hand on a better community than it inherited.

Size has not limited the worldwide reputation that Columbus enjoys for industry, architecture, and an enviable quality of life. Columbus is headquarters for Cummins Engine Company, the world's largest producer of 200 horsepower and above diesel engines, and Arvin Industries, Inc., manufacturer of exhaust systems and ride control products for the international automobile industry. Other companies that started in Columbus and continue to call it home are Cosco Inc., Golden Foundry, and Reeves &

Company. Companies from Japan, Germany, and Canada have added to the community's manufacturing strength by producing automotive and other industrial equipment.

Modern architecture arrived in Columbus in 1942. The congregation of the Tabernacle Christian Church completed their new sanctuary, designed by Eliel Saarinen, a Finnish architect who was a finalist in the competition to design the Chicago Tribune building. Referring to traditional Gothic and Georgian design, Saarinen wrote that "The last drop of expressiveness has been squeezed out of these once so expressive styles." Instead, Saarinen designed a contemporary structure that became one of the first modern churches in America.

After World War II the Columbus population doubled in ten years. In response to the need for schools, Cummins Engine Company, under chairman J. Irwin Miller, made an offer through the company's Foundation that would change the city's horizon. The Foundation would pay the fees for the country's best architects to design the community schools. Thirteen schools have been

designed and built under this program since 1957. The program expanded to other public facilities, including a post office, fire stations, a golf course, and a jail.

Other community groups supported a program of quality design. The congregations of First Baptist Church and St. Peter's Lutheran Church, THE REPUBLIC newspaper, Indiana Bell (now Ameritech), and the library brought in major architects to design their facilities.

Quality design did not stop at buildings. Landscape architects Dan Kiley and Michael Van Valkenburgh added to the Columbus environment. Public art by Henry Moore, Jean Tinguely, J. Seward Johnson, and Dale Chihuly delights adults and children.

As a result of Columbus' concern with its built environment, in 1991 members of the American Institute of Architects ranked Columbus sixth among U.S. cities for its architectural quality, innovation, and design. Only Chicago, New York, Washington, D.C., San Francisco, and Boston ranked higher.

The city's desire for excellence does not stop with its buildings. Community leaders and citizens have worked together to create a quality of life where voluntarism has blossomed. In 1994 Columbus was named an "All-American City." The National Civic League gave the award for outstanding grass-roots action involving public, private, and not-for-profit sectors in identifying and solving critical community issues. Volunteers in Medicine has pulled together representatives from the medical community to provide health care for the working population that is not covered by health insurance. Four Seasons Retirement Home is regularly ranked among the best facilities in the country. Free family programming is a regular event at The Commons. The Hamilton Foundation, as a memorial to B. F. Hamilton, founder of Cosco, Inc., donated Hamilton Center for year-round winter sports recreation.

Columbus is made up of people from all walks of life and many countries. Living in Columbus means you accept a responsibility to care about making the community a better place to live. There is a commitment to save the best of the old and build for the future in a quality way that future generations will consider worth saving.

CONTRIBUTORS

BRENDA ARMSTRONG
BEV BAKER
DONNA BARTHOLD
SHARON BEABOUT
TEREE BERGMAN
LYNN BIGLEY
BOB BISHOP
LORI BLANFORD
JENNIFER BOMBA
RUTH BRASWELL
BETH BRIDGETTS
KIE BRIDGETTS
PAT BRIDGETTS
ELOISE BROWN
MARY BUNIO
GRAZIELLA BUSH
PAT BUSH
GERALDINE BUTZKO
RENE CAMPBELL
SHEILA CARR
DARVEL CHAMBERS
JACQUE CHAMBERS
SIBBY CHAMBERS
MARLENE CHESTNUT
WILMA CHILDRES DOUP
RUTH CHIN
DONNA WILLIAMS-CHRISTIAN
FLETA JONASSEN-COWHERD
JEANEY DAILY
RUTH DAVEE
NORA DELAPP
BARBARA DESMOND
KAY DIETRICH
GENEVIEVE DONICA
ANN ELLIS
LARRY AND CARROL EWERT
BARBARA B. FLAHERTY
NANCY FODREA
CINDY FORCE
MARY LU FOUTS
BARBARA FRAVEL
CINDY FREY
JEANNINE GONSALVES
MARYBELLE GOSSMAN
CHEF JAMES GREGORY
LOIS GRIFFITH
MARIANNE HAMBLEN
BETH HAMILTON

JUANITA HARDEN
LIZ HARPER
DODY HARVEY
LIBBY HAYS
TOOTS HENDERSON
JOANNE HON
JOAN HOPPING
MARIE HUNTINGTON
JILL INGERSOLL
MIKE JAMERSON
DONNA-MARIE KANE
ELAINE K. KEACH
ENID KEMP
SYLVIA KIEL
JENNY KIM
ANN KNOBLOCH
EVAN KNOX
CHRIS LEMLEY
DAVID AND JANE LEWIS
PAT LUCAS
CAREY A. LYNN
RUTH LYNN
NANCY MARBLE
ANDREA R. MARSHALL
JULIA MARSHALL
MARION W. MARSHALL
MICHELE GOLEY MARSHALL
TERIE MCDONALD
JOANN C. MEEK
CAROL MENDENHALL
XENIA MILLER
SAMANTHA MINOR
MARGARET E. NELSON
JEANNETTE NOLAN-WESTLAKE
CINDY OLSON
DENNIS ORWIN
JOYCE ORWIN
SEAN ORWIN
LALITH PARANAVITANA
SUE PARIS
JOAN PEARCY
DENISE PENCE
BOBBIE PITTMAN
DIXIE POE
RON POLLEY
JEAN PRATHER
LINDA D. RHOADES
JUDY RHUDE
JULIA RICHARDS
TERESA RICHMOND
MIKE ROSS

DONNA SASSE
JULIE SCHROEDER
JOANN SCHWARTZKOPF
MARTY SEBASTIAN
JOANNE SEITZ
ROBERT SHEEDY
JODY SHINN
KATHERINE SHORES
MARISSA BRIDGETTS SINDELAR
MARY LOU SLATTERY
CHERYL SMALL
YOKO STAHL
SHERRY STARK
ELAINE STEED
BARBARA STEWART
EDNA THAYER
EILEEN THOMAS
LORI THOMAS
SHIRLEY C. THOMAS
VICKY THOMASSON
JENS THOMSEN
WANDA TREMBACK
NANCY WAGNER
KATHY WALL
PEGGY WAMPLER
SHIRLEY WEERTS
SUZAN WESCOTT
JEANNE WHEELER
MAXINE WHEELER
CARYN WIGGINS
BRET WILLIAMS
MARY ANN WILLIAMSON
JACQUELINE WILSON
CINDY WINTERROWD
MADONNA YATES
PARK YORK
BENVENUTI
COLUMBUS BAR
COLUMBUS INN TEA ROOM
COOKS & COMPANY
FIRST UNITED METHODIST
   CHURCH COOKBOOK
4TH STREET BAR
HUMAN RIGHTS COMMISSION
OTTER CREEK GOLF COURSE
PHI BETA PSI SORORITY
RUDDICK-NUGENT HOUSE
SUPER 8 MOTEL
TRI KAPPA—TAU CHAPTER

APPETIZERS AND SNACKS

APPETIZERS AND SNACKS

CONTENTS

INTERIOR STAIRWELL BEHIND
TWO-STORY GLASS WINDOWS OF
THE COLUMBUS CITY HALL, 1981,
SKIDMORE, OWINGS, & MERRILL.
EDWARD CHARLES BASSETT,
PRINCIPAL ARCHITECT.

CHEESE PUFFS

3 ounces cream cheese

4 ounces sharp cheese, shredded

$^1/_2$ cup butter or margarine

2 egg whites, stiffly beaten

1 loaf bakery bread, crust trimmed, cubed

MELT the cream cheese, sharp cheese and butter in a double boiler. Let cool. Fold the cheese mixture into the egg whites in a bowl. Stir in the bread cubes with 2 forks. Arrange on a waxed paper-lined baking sheet, separating the bread cubes. Chill, loosely covered, overnight. Bake at 400 degrees for 8 minutes. May be frozen before baking for later use. Yield: 20 to 30 servings.

CHEESE STRAWS

8 ounces extra-sharp Cheddar cheese, shredded, at room temperature

1 cup margarine or butter, softened

2 cups flour

$2^1/_2$ cups crisp rice cereal

2 to 3 drops of Worcestershire sauce, or to taste

MIX the cheese, margarine, flour, cereal and Worcestershire sauce in a bowl. Shape into small balls. Place on a nonstick baking sheet. Flatten with a fork. Bake at 350 degrees for 10 minutes. Yield: 15 to 20 servings.

"GOOD LAND, GOOD WATER AND TIMBER," NOTED GENERAL JOHN TIPTON AS HE AND GENERAL JOSEPH BARTHOLOMEW TRAVELED THROUGH THE WHITE RIVER VALLEY IN THE EARLY 1800'S.

APPETIZERS AND SNACKS

CHICKEN WINGS WITH BOURBON

$^1/_2$ cup light soy sauce

$^1/_2$ cup honey

2 tablespoons blended bourbon

2 tablespoons fresh lemon juice

1 teaspoon prepared mustard

$^1/_4$ teaspoon ground ginger

2 pounds chicken wings, disjointed

MIX the soy sauce, honey, bourbon, lemon juice, mustard and ginger in a large shallow bowl. Add the chicken. Chill, covered, overnight. Remove the chicken from the marinade, discarding the remaining marinade. Arrange the chicken on a broiler pan. Broil 5 inches from the heat source until brown and cooked through. Serve hot or cold. May bake at 350 degrees for 30 minutes or until cooked through. Yield: 28 servings.

INDIANA-STYLE CHILES RELLENOS

12 ounces canned chopped green chiles, drained

1 pound sharp Cheddar cheese, shredded

4 eggs

$^1/_2$ teaspoon salt

1 tablespoon chopped cilantro

$^1/_2$ cup flour

2 cups milk

LAYER the chiles and cheese in a 9x13-inch baking pan. Mix the eggs, salt, cilantro, flour and milk in a bowl. Pour over the layers. Bake at 300 degrees for 1 hour.
Yield: 6 to 10 servings.

CRAB MEAT MELTS

2 (6-ounce) cans crab meat

1 cup shredded sharp Cheddar cheese

$1/2$ cup mayonnaise-type salad dressing

2 tablespoons finely chopped red pepper

2 tablespoons sliced green onions

4 drops of hot pepper sauce

$1/4$ teaspoon dillweed

36 Triscuits

MIX the crab meat, cheese, salad dressing, red pepper, green onions, hot pepper sauce and dillweed in a bowl. Spread each cracker with 1 tablespoon of the crab meat mixture. Place on a baking sheet. Bake at 425 degrees for 10 minutes. Yield: 36 servings.

HEALTHY SNACK CRACKERS

2 cups unbleached flour

1 cup toasted wheat germ

3 cups quick-cooking oats

3 tablespoons sugar

1 teaspoon salt

$3/4$ cup safflower oil

1 cup water

1 egg white, lightly beaten

Poppy seeds and sesame seeds to taste

Garlic salt or onion salt to taste

MIX the flour, wheat germ, oats, sugar and salt in a bowl. Add the safflower oil and water, stirring until the dough leaves the side of the bowl. Divide the dough into quarters. Roll each piece into a 10x12-inch rectangle on a lightly floured surface. Roll up loosely. Place on a lightly greased baking sheet. Cut into diamonds, rectangles or squares. Brush with the egg white. Sprinkle with poppy seeds, sesame seeds and garlic salt. Bake at 350 degrees for 15 to 20 minutes or until golden brown. Serve with cheese and fresh fruit. Yield: 8 dozen.

APPETIZERS AND SNACKS

JAPANESE MEATBALLS

1 pound ground beef

1/2 cup soft bread crumbs

1/2 cup finely chopped celery

2 tablespoons corn oil

1/2 cup chopped onion

1 clove of garlic, minced

1 1/2 cups sliced mushrooms

1/2 cup light corn syrup

1/3 cup dry white wine

2 tablespoons soy sauce

2 tablespoons ground ginger

2 teaspoons cornstarch

2 tablespoons water

MIX the ground beef, bread crumbs and celery in a bowl. Shape into 1-inch balls. Heat the corn oil in a large skillet over medium-high heat. Add the meatballs. Cook until brown on all sides. Remove to a platter and keep warm. Drain the skillet, reserving 2 tablespoons drippings. Sauté the onion and garlic in the reserved drippings for 3 minutes.

Add the mushrooms. Cook for 1 minute or until tender. Stir in the corn syrup, wine, soy sauce and ginger. Bring to a boil. Stir in a mixture of the cornstarch and water. Return to a boil over medium heat, stirring constantly. Boil for 1 minute. Pour over the meatballs. Yield: 4 to 5 servings.

OLIVE CHEESE APPETIZERS

3/4 cup flour

1/8 teaspoon salt

1/2 teaspoon paprika

4 ounces sharp Cheddar cheese, shredded

1/4 cup butter, softened

24 to 30 pimento-stuffed green olives

SIFT the flour, salt and paprika together. Mix the cheese and butter in a bowl. Add the flour mixture and mix well. Shape 1 teaspoon of the dough around each olive. Place on a nonstick baking sheet. Bake at 400 degrees for 12 to 15 minutes or until brown. Serve hot. Yield: 24 to 30 servings.

STUFFED MUSHROOMS

2 cups finely chopped corn bread stuffing mix

3/4 cup melted butter or margarine

1 pound fresh mushrooms, stems removed

Parmesan cheese to taste

COMBINE the stuffing mix with enough of the butter to moisten. Spoon into the mushroom caps. Arrange in a circle on a microwave-safe platter. Sprinkle with cheese. Microwave on High until hot and bubbly. Yield: 15 to 20 servings.

PEAR CHEESE APPETIZERS

2 tablespoons lemon juice

2 ripe pears, sliced

4 ounces cream cheese, softened

2 tablespoons crumbled bleu cheese

1 cup chopped pecans

MIX the lemon juice and enough water to cover the pears in a bowl. Add the pears. Let stand for several minutes; drain and pat dry. Spread a mixture of the cream cheese and bleu cheese over one side of each of the pear slices. Coat with pecans. Place on a serving platter. Chill, loosely covered, until serving time. Yield: 4 to 6 servings.

IN 1821 GENERAL JOHN TIPTON GAVE 30 ACRES TO FOUND A TOWN NAMED TIPTONA. THE TOWN PROMPTLY CHANGED THE NAME TO COLUMBUS. THE GENERAL LEFT IN A HUFF AND NEVER CAME BACK.

APPETIZERS and SNACKS

EDNA THAYER'S LEAN SAVORY ONION TART

Edna Thayer, a regional cook and gardener, wrote a "Country Kitchen" feature in THE REPUBLIC newspaper.

1 cup stone-ground whole wheat flour

1 cup unbleached flour

$1/8$ teaspoon salt

$1/3$ cup chilled margarine

$1/3$ cup vegetable oil

Ice water or chilled white wine

2 cups sliced green onions

2 tablespoons margarine

1 tablespoon vegetable oil

1 cup water

1 cup nonfat dry milk powder

$1/2$ cup cottage cheese, drained

1 (8-ounce) package egg substitute

1 tablespoon soy bacon bits, or 1 slice bacon, crisp-cooked, crumbled

Salt and pepper to taste

FOR the crust, sift the whole wheat flour, unbleached flour and $1/8$ teaspoon salt into a bowl. Cut in $1/3$ cup margarine until crumbly. Add $1/3$ cup oil and mix well. Add ice water 1 tablespoon at a time, mixing until a soft dough forms. Roll out on a floured surface and fit into a 10-inch tart pan, trimming and fluting the edge. Line with foil and fill with dried beans. Bake at 400 degrees for 8 minutes. Remove the foil and beans. Bake for 2 minutes longer. For the filling, cook the green onions in 2 tablespoons margarine and 1 tablespoon oil in a skillet until tender. Process 1 cup water, dry milk powder and cottage cheese in a blender until smooth and creamy. Add the egg substitute. Combine with the green onions in a bowl and mix well. Spoon into the baked crust. Sprinkle with the bacon bits. Bake at 400 degrees for 30 minutes. Will serve 2 to 4 as an entrée with a salad and fruit. Yield: 4 to 6 servings.

PEPPERONI ROLL WITH HONEY DIJON DIP

1 (8-count) package refrigerator crescent rolls

2 egg yolks

2 (3-ounce) packages sliced pepperoni

2 egg whites, lightly beaten

2 tablespoons Dijon mustard

2 tablespoons honey

CUT the dough into 2 equal portions. Unroll 1 portion onto a baking sheet, pinching the seams to seal perforations and spreading the dough slightly thinner. Mix the egg yolks in a bowl. Add the pepperoni and stir until the pepperoni is coated. Arrange over the dough on the baking sheet. Unroll the remaining dough on a lightly floured surface, pinching to seal perforations and spreading the dough slightly thinner. Place over the pepperoni layer. Pinch the edges together to seal. Brush with the egg whites. Bake at 375 degrees for 12 to 14 minutes or until brown. Cut into squares. Use a mixture of the Dijon mustard and honey for dipping. Yield: 24 servings.

NEW POTATO APPETIZERS

1$^1/_2$ pounds small new potatoes

1 cup sour cream

4 slices bacon, crisp-cooked, crumbled

$^1/_2$ teaspoon seasoned salt

$^1/_4$ teaspoon pepper

2 teaspoons chives

$^1/_2$ cup shredded Cheddar cheese

COOK the potatoes in water to cover in a saucepan until tender; drain. Cut the potatoes into halves. Scoop out the pulp with a melon baller; discard or reserve for another use. Mix the sour cream, bacon, seasoned salt, pepper and chives in a bowl. Spoon into the potato shells. Top with the cheese. Place on a rack in broiler pan. Broil until the cheese is melted. May be prepared ahead and stored in the refrigerator for up to 24 hours before broiling. Yield: 20 servings.

MONEY WAS RARE AMONG EARLY SETTLERS, SO FOLKS BARTERED. WHISKEY WAS THE MOST COMMON CURRENCY.

APPETIZERS AND SNACKS

PORK ON HORSEBACK

2 tablespoons prepared horseradish

2 tablespoons mayonnaise

1 teaspoon Worcestershire sauce

$^1/_2$ teaspoon salt

8 ounces cream cheese, softened

6 thin slices boiled ham

BEAT the horseradish, mayonnaise, Worcestershire sauce, salt and cream cheese in a mixer bowl until of spreading consistency. Place 1 ham slice on a sheet of waxed paper. Spread with $^1/_5$ of the horseradish mixture. Continue layering with the remaining ham and horseradish mixture, ending with a ham slice. Wrap securely in waxed paper. Freeze for 2 hours to overnight. Cut into small cubes. Spear each cube with a wooden pick. Let stand for 1 hour before serving.

Yield: 36 servings.

QUESADILLA SQUARES

2 cups shredded Cheddar cheese

2 cups shredded Monterey Jack cheese

1 (4-ounce) can whole green chiles, drained, finely chopped

1 cup buttermilk baking mix or low-fat baking mix

4 eggs, beaten, or equivalent amount of egg substitute

2 cups milk

$^1/_4$ cup salsa

SPRINKLE the Cheddar cheese and Monterey Jack cheese in a 9x13-inch glass baking dish sprayed with nonstick cooking spray. Top with the green chiles. Combine the baking mix and eggs in a large mixer bowl. Add the milk, beating until smooth. Pour carefully over the green chiles. Sprinkle the salsa over the top in 2 to 3 lengthwise rows. Bake at 425 degrees for 25 to 30 minutes or until puffed and golden brown. Cool for 10 minutes. Cut into squares. Serve with sour cream, additional salsa and guacamole. For an entrée, serve with refried beans, Spanish rice and/or a red onion and orange salad.

Yield: 12 to 15 servings.

PARTY RYES

1 pound hot sausage

1 pound ground beef

1 pound Velveeta cheese, chopped

1 tablespoon Worcestershire sauce

2 loaves party rye bread

BROWN the sausage and ground beef in an electric skillet, stirring until crumbly; drain well. Add the cheese and Worcestershire sauce. Cook until the cheese is melted, stirring occasionally. Place 1 tablespoon of the mixture on each bread slice. Place on baking sheets. Bake at 350 degrees for 10 minutes. May be frozen for later use before baking. Freeze in zip-top plastic bags.

Yield: 20 to 30 servings.

TORTILLA HAM ROLL-UPS

16 ounces cream cheese, softened

1/2 cup mayonnaise

2 packages dried ham, finely chopped

1 onion, chopped

1 cup shredded Cheddar cheese

Garlic powder to taste

Worcestershire sauce to taste

1 package (10-inch) flour tortillas

MIX the cream cheese, mayonnaise, ham, onion, cheese, garlic powder and Worcestershire sauce in a bowl. Spread a thin layer over each tortilla and roll up. Chill, individually wrapped in plastic wrap, overnight. Slice just before serving. May freeze leftovers.

Yield: 30 to 40 servings.

IN THE 1800'S COLUMBUS BEGAN TO GROW AS A COMMERCIAL CENTER. POWER FROM THE WHITE RIVER DROVE GRIST MILLS, WOOLEN MILLS, AND SAWMILLS. FLATBOATS FROM COLUMBUS TRAVELED AS FAR AS NEW ORLEANS CARRYING CORN, POTATOES, LARD, CHICKENS, LUMBER, AND OTHER GOODS.

APPETIZERS AND SNACKS

FRESH VEGETABLE BARS

2 (8-count) packages refrigerator crescent rolls

16 ounces cream cheese, softened

1 cup mayonnaise-type salad dressing

1 envelope ranch salad dressing mix

1/2 head cauliflower, cut into bite-size pieces

1 bunch broccoli, cut into bite-size pieces

1 carrot, thinly sliced

1 green bell pepper, chopped (optional)

1 cup finely shredded cheese

UNROLL the dough onto a nonstick 12x18-inch baking sheet, sealing the perforations. Bake at 350 degrees for 10 minutes. Cool completely. Mix the cream cheese, salad dressing and salad dressing mix in a bowl. Spread over the crust. Sprinkle with the cauliflower, broccoli, carrot and green pepper and press in lightly. Top with the cheese. Chill, covered, overnight. Cut into bars.
Yield: 24 to 30 servings.

CEREAL MIX

1 1/2 cups unsalted pretzels

3 cups mixed Chex cereal

1/2 cup dry roasted peanuts

2 tablespoons reduced-calorie margarine

1 tablespoon Worcestershire sauce

2 teaspoons Italian seasoning

2 tablespoons grated Parmesan cheese

MIX the pretzels, cereal and peanuts in a large bowl. Heat the margarine, Worcestershire sauce, Italian seasoning and cheese in a small saucepan until the cheese melts, stirring constantly. Pour over the cereal mixture. Spoon into a 9x13-inch baking dish. Bake at 275 degrees for 40 minutes, stirring every 10 minutes. May triple recipe, substituting 1 package corn Chex for the mixed Chex cereal.
Yield: 8 to 9 servings.

ARTICHOKE APPETIZER

1 (14-ounce) can artichoke hearts, drained, chopped

1 (4-ounce) can green chiles, drained, chopped

1 cup mayonnaise

1 cup grated Parmesan cheese

$1/8$ teaspoon Tabasco sauce, or to taste

MIX the artichoke hearts, green chiles, mayonnaise, cheese and Tabasco sauce in a bowl. Spoon into a shallow ovenproof 3-cup bowl. Bake at 300 degrees for 30 minutes. Serve with assorted crackers and thinly sliced heavy bread. Yield: 4 to 6 servings.

HOLIDAY APPETIZER PIE

8 ounces cream cheese, softened

2 tablespoons milk

1 (2-ounce) jar dried beef, chopped

2 tablespoons minced onion

2 tablespoons finely chopped green bell pepper

$1/8$ teaspoon pepper

$1 1/2$ cups sour cream

$1/4$ cup chopped walnuts

COMBINE the cream cheese and milk in a bowl and blend well. Add the beef, onion, green pepper and pepper and mix well. Stir in the sour cream. Spoon into an 8-inch pie plate or shallow baking dish. Sprinkle with the walnuts. Bake at 350 degrees for 15 to 20 minutes or until heated through. Serve with melba rounds and assorted crackers.
Yield: 2 cups.

"THESE PEOPLE . . . ARE BRIMFUL OF ENTERPRISE AND ENERGY, AND BELIEVE AND LIVE IN THE SPIRIT OF PROGRESS."
—FROM THE **LOUISVILLE COURIER-JOURNAL**, AT THE DEDICATION OF THE BARTHOLOMEW COUNTY COURTHOUSE IN 1874

APPETIZERS AND SNACKS

BEER CHEESE

2 pounds Velveeta cheese, chopped

1 small jar chopped pimento

$1/2$ cup finely chopped onion

1 cup flat beer

PROCESS the cheese, pimento and onion in a blender or food processor until mixed. Add the beer. Process until smooth. Chill thoroughly. Serve at room temperature with pretzels or breadsticks. Yield: 15 to 20 servings.

MINCED CLAM DIP

$1/2$ cup canned minced clams

1 clove of garlic, minced

8 ounces low-fat cream cheese, softened

1 teaspoon lemon juice

1 teaspoon Worcestershire sauce

$1/4$ teaspoon salt, or to taste

$1/8$ teaspoon pepper, or to taste

DRAIN the clams, reserving 1 to 2 tablespoons liquid; set aside. Stir the garlic into the cream cheese in a bowl. Add the lemon juice, Worcestershire sauce, salt and pepper. Stir in the clams. Add enough of the reserved liquid to make of desired consistency. Chill for several hours. Serve with assorted crackers. Yield: 12 to 15 servings.

ON A HOT JULY AFTERNOON IN 1844, THE FIRST PASSENGER TRAIN CHUGGED ITS WAY TO COLUMBUS FROM MADISON, INDIANA, AND THE WHOLE TOWN TURNED OUT FOR A GRAND WELCOME. MANY WHO ATTENDED HAD NEVER SEEN A TRAIN.

CRAB MEAT CHEESE BALL

32 ounces cream cheese, softened, mashed

4 green onions, chopped

8 ounces mild Colby cheese, shredded

2 (8-ounce) packages imitation crab meat

Chopped celery (optional)

$1/2$ teaspoon salt

$1/8$ teaspoon pepper

1 package saltines

1 teaspoon seasoned salt

MIX the cream cheese, green onions, Colby cheese, crab meat, celery, salt and pepper in a bowl. Shape into a ball. Crush some of the crackers in a zip-top plastic bag. Add the seasoned salt and shake until mixed. Roll the cheese ball in the crumbs. Garnish with pitted Spanish olives. Chill for 2 hours. Serve chilled with the remaining saltines.
Yield: 20 to 25 servings.

CRAB GRASS

$1/4$ cup butter

1 small onion, finely chopped

1 (6-ounce) can crab meat, drained

$1/4$ cup freshly grated Parmesan cheese

1 (10-ounce) package frozen chopped spinach, cooked, drained

MELT the butter in a skillet. Add the onion. Cook until translucent. Combine with the crab meat, cheese and spinach in a bowl and mix well. Serve warm with rye bread and round party crackers. Yield: 15 to 20 servings.

COLUMBUS WAS A TOWN WHERE ENTREPRENEURS COULD MAKE THEIR MARK. IN 1849 FARMER FRANCIS J. CRUMP BEGAN LENDING MONEY. HE WAS OFTEN SEEN WITH PAPERS STICKING FROM HIS HAT BRIM. HIS "OFFICE IN A HAT" DID WELL ENOUGH TO BECOME THE TOWN'S FIRST NATIONAL BANK.

APPETIZERS AND SNACKS

CHUTNEY CHEESE BALL

8 ounces cream cheese, softened

1 teaspoon curry powder

$1/2$ cup chopped Major Grey's chutney

$1/4$ teaspoon dry mustard

Paprika to taste

Chopped unsalted peanuts

BEAT the cream cheese, curry powder, chutney and mustard in a mixer bowl until creamy. Chill slightly. Shape into a ball. Sprinkle with paprika and coat with peanuts. Serve with crackers. Best if prepared in advance to allow flavors to blend. Yield: 15 to 20 servings.

SHIRLEY'S ITALIAN CHEESE BALL OR PINWHEELS

8 ounces cream cheese, softened

8 ounces mozzarella cheese, shredded

5 green onions, chopped

$1/2$ cup sliced black olives

Garlic powder and basil to taste

Rosemary and thyme to taste

Wine (optional)

4 (10-inch) flour tortillas (optional)

MIX the cream cheese and mozzarella cheese in a medium bowl. Stir in the green onions, black olives, garlic powder, basil, rosemary and thyme, thinning with a small amount of wine if needed. For Cheese Ball, wrap in plastic wrap. Place in a bowl to shape into a ball. Chill, wrapped in plastic wrap, until serving time. Serve with crackers. For Pinwheels, spread the cream cheese mixture over the tortillas. Roll up. Chill, individually wrapped in plastic wrap, for 2 hours or longer. Slice to serve. Yield: 6 to 8 servings.

THE TOWN'S FIRST SAFE WAS IN JOSEPH I. IRWIN'S DRY GOODS STORE, WHERE FARMERS WOULD LEAVE THEIR MONEY "ON DEPOSIT." AFTER THE STORE WAS SOLD, IRWIN'S BANK TOOK ITS PLACE IN 1871. THIS WAS THE FORERUNNER OF THE IRWIN FINANCIAL CORPORATION.

MEXICAN DIP

1 can refried beans

2 cups sour cream

1 envelope taco seasoning mix

1 pound ground beef

1 package shredded cheese

1 large tomato, chopped

Chopped green onions (optional)

SPREAD the beans in a 9x9-inch pan. Spread a mixture of the sour cream and seasoning mix over the beans. Brown the ground beef in a skillet, stirring until crumbly; drain. Spread over the sour cream layer. Sprinkle with the cheese. Add the tomato, green onions and/or other favorite toppings. Serve with tortilla chips. Yield: 8 to 12 servings.

VIDALIA ONION STARTER

1 cup mayonnaise

8 ounces Swiss cheese, shredded

8 ounces Vidalia onions, chopped

MIX the mayonnaise, cheese and onions in a bowl. Spoon into a baking dish. Bake at 350 degrees for 30 to 45 minutes or until heated through and golden brown. Serve with sturdy crackers. Yield: 15 to 20 servings.

THE LUCAS-MARR BUILDING AT 422-26 WASHINGTON STREET WAS BUILT IN 1887 FOR ELIZABETH LUCAS, THE FIRST FEMALE BANK PRESIDENT IN INDIANA.

APPETIZERS AND SNACKS

CINDY'S PESTO SPREAD

2 tablespoons olive oil

7 to 8 fresh basil leaves

2 cloves of garlic, crushed

$1/4$ cup walnuts or pine nuts

$1/4$ cup grated Parmesan cheese

8 ounces cream cheese, softened

COMBINE the olive oil, basil, garlic, walnuts and Parmesan cheese in a food processor container. Process until finely chopped. Add the cream cheese. Process until smooth. Spoon into a bowl. Garnish with a fresh sprig of basil. Serve with crusty bread or fresh vegetables. Yield: 8 to 10 servings.

ROASTED RED PEPPER SPREAD

1 small or medium red bell pepper, cut into halves, seeded

2 cloves of garlic, crushed

4 to 5 fresh basil leaves

$1/4$ cup grated Parmesan cheese (optional)

8 ounces cream cheese, softened

PLACE the red pepper skin side up in a baking pan. Bake at 350 degrees for 40 minutes or until the skin begins to turn dark and bubble. Let cool and peel. Combine the garlic, basil, Parmesan cheese and red pepper in a food processor container. Process for 5 to 10 seconds or until chopped. Add the cream cheese. Process until smooth. Serve with very thinly sliced crusty bread.
Yield: 8 to 10 servings.

IN 1864 JOHN V. STOREY, A LOCAL DRUGGIST, HIRED JAMES V. PERKINSON TO BUILD A HOME AT 506 FIFTH STREET. IN 1973, WHEN THE CITY RECOGNIZED THE NEED FOR AN INFORMATION CENTER TO HOST THE INCREASING NUMBER OF VISITORS ATTRACTED TO THIS "SHOWCASE OF MODERN ARCHITECTURE," THE STOREY HOME WAS RENOVATED AND BECAME THE VISITORS CENTER.

RADISH DIP

8 ounces cream cheese, softened

$1/4$ cup butter or margarine, softened

1 cup grated radishes

$1/4$ cup finely grated onion

$1/2$ teaspoon celery salt

$1/8$ teaspoon paprika, or to taste

$1/2$ teaspoon Worcestershire sauce

PROCESS the cream cheese, butter, radishes, onion, celery salt, paprika and Worcestershire sauce in a food processor until mixed. Spoon into a serving bowl. Chill, covered, thoroughly. Serve with assorted crackers. Add a small amount of milk to the mixture if a food processor is not available for mixing.
Yield: 8 to 10 servings.

ROUND OF RYE DIP

1 round loaf rye bread

$1^1/3$ cups sour cream

$1^1/3$ cups mayonnaise

2 teaspoons Beau Monde seasoning

2 tablespoons dill seeds

2 teaspoons onion flakes

2 teaspoons parsley flakes

HOLLOW out the center of the bread. Cut the removed bread into cubes. Mix the sour cream, mayonnaise, Beau Monde seasoning, dill seeds, onion flakes and parsley flakes in a bowl. Spoon into the center of the bread. Place on a large platter and surround with the bread cubes. Yield: 15 to 20 servings.

THE FINE QUEEN ANNE-STYLE HOME AT 605 FIFTH STREET WAS DESIGNED BY LOCAL ARCHITECT CHARLES F. SPARRELL IN 1891 FOR DR. J. WILL PRALL. SPARRELL ALSO DESIGNED THE CITY HALL IN 1895 AND THE GARFIELD SCHOOL IN 1896. CITY HALL SERVED THE COMMUNITY WELL UNTIL 1981. IT HAS BEEN RENOVATED AND NOW HOUSES THE COLUMBUS INN. IT IS LISTED ON THE NATIONAL REGISTER OF HISTORIC PLACES. THE GARFIELD SCHOOL HAS BEEN RENOVATED BY ARVIN INDUSTRIES, INC. THE RENOVATION WAS FEATURED IN THE MAY/JUNE 1991 ISSUE OF **HISTORIC PRESERVATION** MAGAZINE.

APPETIZERS AND SNACKS

CATHY'S SALSA

2 (28-ounce) cans tomatoes, drained

1 bunch cilantro, stems removed, rinsed

1 to 2 bunches green onions, chopped

1 small can chopped green chiles

1 tablespoon dried oregano, or
3 tablespoons fresh

Onion salt to taste

Tabasco sauce to taste

PROCESS 1 can of the tomatoes in a food processor until coarsely chopped. Pour into a large bowl. Process the remaining tomatoes with the cilantro in a food processor until less coarsely chopped but not puréed. Add the tomato mixture, green onions, green chiles, oregano, onion salt and Tabasco sauce to the bowl and mix well. Serve with tortilla chips. Yield: 25 to 30 servings.

GRACE'S SHRIMP DIP

2 (6-ounce) cans baby shrimp, drained

8 ounces cream cheese, softened

1/2 cup chopped celery

4 teaspoons prepared horseradish

2 tablespoons chopped onion

2 tablespoons catsup

MIX the shrimp, cream cheese, celery, horse-radish, onion and catsup in a bowl. Chill, covered, until serving time. Serve with assorted crackers. Yield: 15 to 20 servings.

JILL'S TEENAGE DIP

4 (4-ounce) cans chicken

4 (8-ounce) jars taco sauce

2 envelopes taco seasoning mix

2 (4-ounce) cans chopped black olives

4 cups shredded Cheddar cheese

MIX the chicken, taco sauce, seasoning mix, olives and cheese in a bowl. Spoon into 2 baking dishes. Bake at 350 degrees for 20 minutes. Serve with tortilla chips.
Yield: 30 to 40 servings.

ZESTY TOMATO DIP

1 (3-ounce) package lemon gelatin

$^1/_2$ cup boiling water

16 ounces cream cheese, softened

1 (10-ounce) can tomato soup

1 cup mayonnaise-type salad dressing or mayonnaise

$^1/_2$ cup chopped green onions

$^1/_2$ cup chopped bell pepper

DISSOLVE the gelatin in the boiling water. Mix with the cream cheese, soup, salad dressing, green onions and bell pepper in a bowl. Serve warm as a dip or chill and serve as a spread. May be frozen; thaw before using.
Yield: 30 to 40 servings.

IN 1877 THE REVEREND Z. T. SWEENEY, PASTOR OF THE CHRISTIAN CHURCH IN COLUMBUS, FELT A NEW CHURCH BUILDING WAS DESPERATELY NEEDED. HE DECIDED TO TAKE DRASTIC ACTION. ONE SUNDAY, WITHOUT WARNING, HE ASKED ALL USHERS TO LOCK THE CHURCH DOORS WHILE HE ANNOUNCED THAT THE DOORS WOULD NOT BE OPENED UNTIL $10,000 WAS COLLECTED. IT WORKED, AND THE CONGREGATION HAD THE MONEY FOR ITS NEW TABERNACLE CHRISTIAN CHURCH, WHICH WAS BUILT ON LAFAYETTE AT SIXTH STREET. THIS SAME CONGREGATION AGAIN NEEDED A NEW BUILDING NOT TOO MANY YEARS LATER, AND THE FIRST CHRISTIAN CHURCH WAS BUILT.

APPETIZERS AND SNACKS

TUNA SPREAD

1 (12-ounce) can tuna, drained

1 (8-ounce) can sliced water chestnuts, drained

1 cup mayonnaise

2 tablespoons chopped onion

2 teaspoons lemon juice

2 teaspoons soy sauce

1 teaspoon curry powder

COMBINE the tuna, water chestnuts, mayonnaise, onion, lemon juice, soy sauce and curry powder in a bowl and mix well. Chill, covered, until serving time. Serve with assorted crackers. May also be used as a spread for sandwiches. Yield: 30 to 40 servings.

HOT SAUCE FOR CHICKEN WINGS

1^1/$_2$ cups butter

^{1}/$_4$ cup vinegar

^{1}/$_4$ cup lemon juice

^{1}/$_4$ cup hot sauce

^{1}/$_4$ cup Tabasco sauce

^{1}/$_4$ cup Worcestershire sauce

Garlic powder and onion powder to taste

MELT the butter in a saucepan. Add the vinegar, lemon juice, hot sauce, Tabasco sauce and Worcestershire sauce and mix well. Simmer for 1 hour, stirring occasionally. Stir in with garlic powder and onion powder. Keeps for 1 month in the refrigerator. To use, toss cooked chicken wings with the sauce until coated. Yield: 2^1/$_2$ cups.

COLONEL ISAAC M. BROWN ISSUED THE FIRST DAILY FOUR-PAGE NEWSPAPER, **THE EVENING REPUBLICAN,** ON NOVEMBER 12, 1877. DURING THE 1800S NEWSPAPERS BEGAN THE TRANSFORMATION TO WHAT WE READ TODAY. **THE REPUBLIC,** COLUMBUS' DAILY PAPER, IS STILL OWNED BY THE SAME FAMILY.

BREAKFAST AND BREADS

BREAKFAST AND BREADS

CONTENTS

LOOKING DOWN INTO THE
LIBRARY OF CLIFTY CREEK
ELEMENTARY SCHOOL, 1982,
DESIGNED BY RICHARD MEIER
& PARTNERS.

AUNT WINNIE POO'S FAVORITE BREAD

2 envelopes yeast or rapid-rise yeast

2 cups warm (105 to 115 degrees) water

$^1/_2$ cup sugar

1 tablespoon salt

2 large eggs, or equivalent amount of egg substitute

$^1/_4$ cup vegetable oil

6 to 6$^1/_2$ cups flour

$^1/_2$ cup wheat germ

$^1/_2$ cup wheat bran

DISSOLVE the yeast in the water in a large mixer bowl. Stir in the sugar, salt, eggs, oil and 3 cups of the flour. Beat until smooth. Add the wheat germ, wheat bran and enough of the remaining flour to make a soft dough. Knead with the dough hook for 8 to 10 minutes or until smooth and elastic. Place in a greased bowl, turning to grease the surface. Let rise, covered, in a warm place for 1 hour or until doubled in bulk. Punch the dough down. Divide into halves. Roll each half into a 9x18-inch rectangle on a lightly floured surface. Roll up from the short side, pressing to seal the ends and folding the ends under the loaves. Place seam side down in 2 greased 5x9-inch loaf pans. Brush with additional oil. Let rise for 1 hour or until doubled. Bake at 375 degrees for 30 to 35 minutes or until the loaves are light brown and sound hollow when tapped on the bottom. Remove to wire racks to cool. Yield: 20 to 24 servings.

LOW-FAT BANANA BREAD

1$^3/_4$ cups flour

1$^1/_4$ teaspoons baking powder

$^1/_2$ teaspoon baking soda

$^2/_3$ cup sugar

1 teaspoon vanilla extract

$^1/_3$ cup applesauce

2 egg whites

2 tablespoons skim milk

1 cup mashed bananas

MIX the flour, baking powder, baking soda and sugar in a bowl. Add the vanilla, applesauce, egg whites, skim milk and bananas and mix until moistened. Spoon into a greased and floured loaf pan. Bake at 350 degrees for 1 hour or until the loaf tests done.
Yield: 10 to 12 servings.

BREAKFAST AND BREADS

COCOA BANANA BREAD

2 cups flour

$^1/_3$ cup baking cocoa

1 teaspoon baking soda

$^1/_2$ teaspoon salt

$^1/_2$ cup butter or margarine, softened

1 cup sugar

1 cup mashed bananas

$^1/_4$ cup milk

2 eggs

1 teaspoon vanilla extract

$^1/_2$ cup chopped pecans or walnuts

MIX the flour, cocoa, baking soda and salt together. Combine the butter, sugar, bananas, milk, eggs and vanilla in a mixer bowl. Beat at medium speed for 1 minute. Add the flour mixture, stirring until moistened. Stir in the pecans. Spoon into a greased loaf pan. Bake at 350 degrees for 50 to 60 minutes or until the loaf tests done. Cool in the pan for 5 minutes. Remove to a wire rack to cool completely. Yield: 10 to 12 servings.

DILLY CASSEROLE BREAD

1 envelope yeast

$^1/_4$ cup warm water

1 cup cottage cheese or low-fat cottage cheese

2 tablespoons sugar

1 tablespoon minced onion

1 tablespoon butter

2 tablespoons dillseeds

1 teaspoon salt

$^1/_4$ teaspoon baking soda

1 egg

$2^1/_4$ to $2^1/_2$ cups flour

Melted butter

SOFTEN the yeast in the water. Heat the cottage cheese to lukewarm. Mix the cottage cheese, sugar, onion, butter, dillseeds, salt, baking soda, egg and yeast mixture in a bowl. Add enough flour gradually to form a stiff dough, beating well after each addition. Let rise, covered, in a warm place until doubled in bulk. Punch down. Place in a greased 2-quart casserole. Let rise until almost doubled. Bake at 350 degrees for 40 to 50 minutes or until the loaf tests done. Brush the top with butter. May sprinkle with additional salt. Yield: 8 to 12 servings.

FLAT BREAD

1 envelope dry yeast

$1/2$ cup warm (110 to 115 degrees) water

$1/3$ cup sugar

2 tablespoons vegetable oil

1 tablespoon salt

$1/2$ cup rye flour or whole wheat flour

$5^1/2$ to 6 cups all-purpose flour

$1^1/2$ cups warm (110 to 115 degrees) water

DISSOLVE the yeast in $1/2$ cup water in a large bowl. Add the sugar, oil, salt, rye flour, 3 cups of the all-purpose flour and $1^1/2$ cups water and beat until smooth. Add enough of the remaining all-purpose flour to make a soft dough. Knead on a floured board for 6 to 8 minutes or until smooth and elastic. Place in a greased bowl, turning to grease the surface. Let rise, covered, in a warm place for 1 hour or until doubled in bulk. Punch the dough down. Divide into halves and place on a greased baking sheet. Flatten each to $1/2$-inch thickness. Pierce each loaf several times with a fork. Let rise, covered, for 30 minutes or until almost doubled. Bake at 375 degrees for 25 to 30 minutes or until golden brown.
Yield: 20 to 24 servings.

FIG BAR BREAD

$1^1/2$ cups sifted flour

$2/3$ cup sugar

$1^1/2$ teaspoons baking powder

$1/2$ teaspoon salt

2 eggs, beaten

$1/2$ cup milk

$1/3$ cup vegetable oil

$1/2$ teaspoon vanilla extract

$1/3$ cup packed brown sugar

$1/2$ teaspoon cinnamon

2 tablespoons butter or margarine

6 to 7 fig bars, crumbled (1 cup)

SIFT the flour, sugar, baking powder and salt into a large bowl. Mix the eggs, milk, oil and vanilla in a medium bowl. Add to the flour mixture and blend well. Combine the brown sugar and cinnamon in a small bowl. Cut in the butter until crumbly. Stir in the cookie crumbs. Pour $1/3$ of the batter into a greased and floured loaf pan. Sprinkle with half the crumb mixture. Repeat the layers. Top with the remaining batter. Swirl gently with a narrow spatula to marbleize. Bake at 350 degrees for 50 to 55 minutes or until the loaf tests done. Cool in the pan for 5 minutes. Remove to a wire rack to cool completely.
Yield: 10 to 12 servings.

BREAKFAST AND BREADS

FOCACCIA

2 envelopes dry yeast

2 cups water (90 degrees)

2 tablespoons sugar

$^1/_4$ cup olive oil

$^1/_2$ cup vegetable oil

1 teaspoon salt

5$^1/_2$ cups flour

$^1/_4$ cup olive oil

6 cloves of garlic, crushed

DISSOLVE the yeast in the water. Pour into a food processor container. Add the sugar, $^1/_4$ cup olive oil, vegetable oil and salt. Add 3 cups of the flour. Process for 5 minutes or until the dough begins to pull away from the side of the container. Add the remaining flour. Process until smooth. Divide the dough into halves. Place each half on an oiled 13x18-inch baking sheet. Press the dough to the edges of the pans. Let rise for 30 minutes. Brush with a mixture of $^1/_4$ cup olive oil and garlic. Bake at 375 degrees for 30 minutes. Yield: 20 to 24 servings.

SPICY PINEAPPLE BREAD

1$^1/_2$ cups all-purpose flour

1$^1/_2$ cups whole wheat flour

2 teaspoons baking soda

1 teaspoon salt

$^1/_2$ teaspoon baking powder

1$^1/_2$ teaspoons cinnamon

$^3/_4$ teaspoon nutmeg

1 cup chopped pecans or walnuts

1 cup raisins

2 eggs

1 cup vegetable oil

$^1/_3$ cup sugar

2 teaspoons vanilla extract

2 cups grated zucchini

1 (8-ounce) can crushed pineapple, drained

MIX the all-purpose flour, whole wheat flour, baking soda, salt, baking powder, cinnamon, nutmeg, pecans and raisins in a medium bowl. Beat the eggs in a large bowl. Add the oil, sugar and vanilla and beat until thick and foamy. Stir in the zucchini and pineapple. Add the flour mixture, stirring just until mixed. Spoon into 2 greased and floured loaf pans. Bake at 350 degrees for 45 minutes. Yield: 14 servings.

HERB MOTHER'S PESTO BREAD

1 1/2 envelopes dry yeast

1 tablespoon sugar

2 cups warm (105 to 115 degrees) water

6 to 7 cups flour

1 1/2 teaspoons salt

2 cups chopped fresh basil

1/2 cup chopped fresh parsley

1/2 cup olive oil

2 cloves of garlic, minced or pressed

1/4 cup grated Parmesan cheese

STIR the yeast and a large pinch of the sugar into the water in a 2-cup measure. Let stand until bubbly and foamy. Combine 2 cups of the flour, salt and remaining sugar in a large bowl. Beat in the yeast mixture. Add the remaining flour 1 cup at a time until a soft dough forms, mixing well after each addition. Knead on a floured board until smooth and elastic. Place in an oiled bowl, turning to grease the surface. Let rise, covered, for 1 1/2 hours. Turn onto a floured board. Punch the dough down. Divide the dough into halves. Pat each half into a 10x12-inch rectangle. Mix the basil, parsley, olive oil, garlic and cheese in a bowl. Spread a thin layer of the pesto over the rectangles, leaving a 1-inch border. Roll each piece of dough into a cylinder, starting at the long side. Shape into loaves. Let rise for 5 minutes. Place the loaves on a baking sheet sprinkled with cornmeal. Brush the loaves with cold water. Place a pan of boiling water in the oven. Bake the loaves at 400 degrees for 35 to 40 minutes or until golden brown. Cool on a wire rack.
Yield: 20 to 24 servings.

BREAKFAST *and* BREADS

PUMPKIN BREAD

3^1/$_2$ cups flour

1 teaspoon baking powder

2 teaspoons salt

1 teaspoon cinnamon

1 teaspoon nutmeg

1 teaspoon allspice

^{1}/$_2$ teaspoon ground cloves

3 cups sugar

4 eggs, beaten

1 cup vegetable oil

1 (16-ounce) can pumpkin

^{2}/$_3$ cup water

SIFT the flour, baking powder, salt, cinnamon, nutmeg, allspice and cloves together. Mix the sugar, eggs and oil in a large bowl. Add the pumpkin. Add the flour mixture and mix well. Stir in the water. Spoon into 2 greased and floured loaf pans. Bake at 350 degrees for 1 hour. Yield: 20 to 24 servings.

GREAT-GREAT-GRANDMOTHER KIEL'S RAISIN BREAD

1 cup raisins

2 cups water

^{1}/$_2$ cup margarine

1 cup sugar

1 teaspoon cinnamon

1 teaspoon nutmeg

^{1}/$_2$ teaspoon ground cloves

1 teaspoon baking soda

1 teaspoon baking powder

3 cups flour

COMBINE the raisins, water, margarine and sugar in a saucepan. Boil for 5 minutes. Let cool. Mix the cinnamon, nutmeg, cloves, baking soda, baking powder and flour in a bowl. Add the raisin mixture and mix well. Spoon into a greased and floured loaf pan. Bake at 325 degrees for 1 to 1^1/$_2$ hours or until the loaf is dark brown and raised in the center. The loaf may start to crack in the center and the sides may pull away from the pan. Cool in the pan on a wire rack for several minutes. Remove to a wire rack to cool completely. Yield: 10 to 12 servings.

WALNUT BREAD

This recipe came from architect Eliot Noyes.

    2 eggs, beaten

    1 cup sugar

    2 cups milk

    4 cups flour

    2 teaspoons (heaping) baking powder

    Salt to taste

    1 cup chopped walnuts

COMBINE the eggs, sugar, milk, flour, baking powder and salt in a bowl and mix well. Stir in the walnuts. Spoon into 2 greased and floured loaf pans. Let rise for 20 minutes. Bake at 325 to 350 degrees for 45 minutes or until the loaves test done. Serve thinly sliced and spread with butter for lunch or tea, or toast for breakfast. Yield: 20 to 24 servings.

ANGEL BISCUITS

    1 envelope yeast

    $^1/_2$ cup warm (110 to 115 degrees) water

    5 cups flour

    1 teaspoon salt

    1 teaspoon baking soda

    1 tablespoon baking powder

    3 tablespoons sugar

    $^3/_4$ cup (scant) shortening

    2 cups buttermilk

DISSOLVE the yeast in the water in a small bowl. Mix the flour, salt, baking soda, baking powder and sugar in a large bowl. Cut in the shortening until crumbly. Add the buttermilk and yeast mixture, mixing until moistened. Chill, covered, until needed. Remove the needed amount of dough; unused dough can be kept refrigerated for later use. Roll $^1/_2$ inch thick on a floured surface. Cut with a biscuit cutter. Place on a greased baking sheet. Bake at 400 degrees for 12 minutes. Yield: 6 dozen.

ELIOT NOYES OF NEW CAANAN, CONNECTICUT, DESIGNED THE SOUTHSIDE ELEMENTARY SCHOOL IN 1969. SOUTHSIDE HAS UNUSUAL WINDOW AND DOOR TREATMENTS AND JUTTING PARAPETS. THE MAIN ENTRANCE OF THE SCHOOL OPENS INTO THE COMMONS IN THE CENTER UNDERNEATH A TWO-STORY SKYLIGHT AREA. TO MEET THE CHANGING EDUCATIONAL NEEDS OF THE COMMUNITY, THE BUILDING, FORMERLY A JUNIOR HIGH SCHOOL, WAS CONVERTED TO AN ELEMENTARY SCHOOL IN 1983.

BREAKFAST *AND* BREADS

BETTY'S REAL SOUTHERN BISCUITS

2 cups self-rising flour

$1/8$ teaspoon baking soda

1 tablespoon (rounded) shortening

1 cup buttermilk

MIX the flour and baking soda in a bowl. Add the shortening and mix well. Add the buttermilk, mixing until smooth. Place on a floured board and sprinkle with additional flour. Knead slightly. Roll out and cut with a biscuit cutter. Place on a baking sheet. Broil until the biscuit tops are brown. Place the baking sheet on the lowest oven rack. Bake at 500 degrees for 10 to 15 minutes or until the bottoms of the biscuits are brown. Yield: 4 servings.

STICKY CINNAMON ROLLS

1 cup chopped pecans

2 loaves frozen bread dough, thawed

$1/2$ cup melted butter or margarine

1 (6-ounce) package vanilla pudding and pie filling mix

1 tablespoon milk

1 cup packed brown sugar

1 tablespoon cinnamon

SPRINKLE the pecans in a greased 9x13-inch baking pan. Shape the dough into 1-inch balls. Arrange in a single layer in the prepared pan. Heat the butter, pudding mix, milk, brown sugar and cinnamon in a saucepan. Pour over the dough. Let rise, loosely covered, in the refrigerator overnight. Bake at 350 degrees for 30 minutes. Invert immediately onto a foil-lined baking sheet.

Yield: 8 to 10 servings.

AMERICA FIRST DISCOVERED COLUMBUS IN HORSE AND BUGGY DAYS. WILLIAM MOONEY AND SONS SUPPLIED A NATIONAL MARKET WITH HARNESSES AND BELTS. REEVES & COMPANY, ORIGINALLY A MANUFACTURER OF AGRICULTURAL MACHINERY, DEVELOPED THE VARIABLE TRANSMISSION. THE AMERICAN STARCH COMPANY ON WASHINGTON STREET, FOUNDED IN 1881, BECAME THE LARGEST STARCH PRODUCER IN THE UNITED STATES, USING 2,500 BUSHELS OF CORN A DAY.

CURRANT SCONES

1 cup dried currants

3 tablespoons brandy or sherry

4$\frac{1}{2}$ cups flour

2 teaspoons baking powder

$\frac{1}{2}$ teaspoon baking soda

2 tablespoons sugar

1 cup unsalted butter

1 cup whipping cream

SOAK the currants in the brandy until plumped; drain. Sift the flour, baking powder, baking soda and sugar into a bowl. Cut in the butter with a pastry cutter or in a food processor. Stir in the whipping cream, mixing until the dough holds together. Add the currants. Wrap in plastic wrap and chill. Roll $\frac{3}{4}$ inch thick on a floured board. Cut into 2$\frac{1}{2}$-inch rounds. Place close together on a lightly buttered baking sheet. Bake at 375 degrees for 13 to 15 minutes or until puffed and golden brown. May brush tops with additional whipping cream for a glazed finish. Yield: 15 to 20 servings.

CARROT WALNUT MUFFINS

2 cups flour

1$\frac{1}{3}$ cups sugar

2 teaspoons baking soda

1 teaspoon cinnamon

$\frac{1}{4}$ teaspoon salt

2 cups grated carrots

$\frac{1}{2}$ cup raisins

$\frac{1}{2}$ cup chopped walnuts

1 (8-ounce) can crushed pineapple, drained

3 eggs

1 cup vegetable oil

2 teaspoons vanilla extract

MIX the flour, sugar, baking soda, cinnamon and salt in a large bowl. Stir in the carrots, raisins, walnuts and pineapple. Beat the eggs lightly in a medium bowl. Stir in the oil and vanilla. Add the egg mixture to the flour mixture, stirring just until moistened. Fill greased or paper-lined muffin cups $\frac{2}{3}$ full with batter. Bake at 350 degrees for 25 minutes or until golden brown. Remove immediately from the muffin cups. Yield: 20 to 22 servings.

BREAKFAST AND BREADS

BROCCOLI CORN BREAD

1 (10-ounce) package frozen chopped broccoli, cooked, drained

1 cup cottage cheese

1 large onion, chopped

4 eggs

$1/2$ cup margarine, softened

1 (9-ounce) package corn muffin mix

MIX the broccoli, cottage cheese, onion, eggs, margarine and corn muffin mix in a bowl. Spoon into a greased 9x13-inch baking pan or glass baking dish. Bake at 350 degrees for 45 minutes or until golden brown. Freezes well. Yield: 12 to 15 servings.

ROSEMARY ORANGE MARMALADE

5 sprigs of fresh rosemary

2 cups boiling water

4 to 5 oranges

3 cups sugar

3 ounces liquid pectin

STEEP 1 sprig of the rosemary in the boiling water for 30 minutes; discard the herb sprig. Peel the zest from the oranges, removing as little pith as possible. Julienne the zest. Combine with water to cover in a saucepan. Simmer, covered, for 30 minutes or until tender; drain and reserve. Free the orange sections from the membranes with a sharp knife. Seed the oranges and chop coarsely. Combine the oranges, rosemary infusion and sugar in a nonreactive saucepan. Boil for 35 minutes, stirring frequently. Add the pectin. Boil for 1 minute. Place 1 sprig of rosemary in each of 4 half-pint jars. Add the marmalade. Seal the jars. Yield: 2 cups.

CRUMB COFFEE CAKE

1 tablespoon dry bread crumbs

2 cups flour

1 cup plus 2 tablespoons sugar

1 teaspoon salt

10 tablespoons unsalted butter, softened

1 teaspoon baking powder

$^1/_2$ teaspoon baking soda

$^3/_4$ cup buttermilk, at room temperature

1 egg, at room temperature

1 teaspoon vanilla extract

3 ounces walnuts or pecans, finely chopped

$^1/_2$ cup packed dark brown sugar

1 teaspoon cinnamon

GREASE the bottom and side of a 10-inch springform pan. Sprinkle the bread crumbs in the pan. Shake lightly to coat; tap out any excess. Whisk the flour, sugar and salt in a large bowl. Cut in the butter with a whisk until crumbly. Remove 1 cup of the mixture to a small bowl. Whisk the baking powder and baking soda into the flour mixture in the large bowl. Add the buttermilk, egg and vanilla, whisking vigorously until thick and smooth. Pour into the pan. Add the walnuts, brown sugar and cinnamon to the reserved flour mixture and toss with a fork. Sprinkle over the batter. Bake at 350 degrees for 50 to 55 minutes or until the center is set. Place the pan on a wire rack and remove the side of the pan. Let stand for 2 hours or until cooled completely. Yield: 8 to 10 servings.

IN 1881 GAFF, GENT AND THOMAS BEGAN MAKING THE FIRST DRY CEREAL, CEREALINE. CEREALINE WAS THE FIRST COLUMBUS PRODUCT TO SELL NATIONWIDE. THIS NEW PRODUCT WAS USED BOTH AS A DRY CEREAL AND AS A MALT SUBSTITUTE IN BREWING. THE CEREALINE MILL BUILDING IS NOW THE CENTERPIECE OF CUMMINS ENGINE COMPANY'S CORPORATE HEADQUARTERS IN DOWNTOWN COLUMBUS.

BREAKFAST AND BREADS

SOUR CREAM COFFEE CAKE

1 cup chopped walnuts

1 tablespoon cinnamon

$^1/_2$ cup sugar

2 cups flour

$^3/_4$ teaspoon salt

1 teaspoon baking powder

1 teaspoon baking soda

$^1/_2$ cup shortening

1 cup sugar

2 eggs

1 cup sour cream

1 teaspoon vanilla extract

COMBINE the walnuts, cinnamon and $^1/_2$ cup sugar in a bowl and mix well. Mix the flour, salt, baking powder and baking soda together. Cream the shortening and 1 cup sugar in a mixer bowl. Add the eggs, sour cream and vanilla and mix well. Add the flour mixture and mix well. Pour half the batter into a nonstick bundt pan. Sprinkle with half the walnut mixture. Spread the remaining batter over the walnut mixture in the pan. Sprinkle with the remaining walnut mixture. Bake at 350 degrees for 35 to 40 minutes or until the coffee cake tests done. Yield: 16 servings.

ON OCTOBER 15, 1896, THE FIRST RURAL FREE MAIL DELIVERY IN INDIANA WAS STARTED. HOPE, INDIANA, CAN BOAST OF HAVING THE OLDEST CONTINUOUSLY OPERATING RURAL DELIVERY SERVICE IN THE COUNTRY. A MUSEUM THAT DISPLAYS LETTERS AND OTHER MEMENTOS OF EARLY MAIL DELIVERY WAS DEDICATED IN HOPE IN 1975.

OVEN PANCAKE FOR FOUR

¹/₄ cup unsalted butter

4 eggs

1 cup milk

1 cup flour

PLACE the butter in a 3-quart baking dish. Bake at 425 degrees just until butter is melted. Process the eggs in a food processor for 1 minute. Add the milk and flour gradually, processing constantly. Pour over the butter in the hot baking dish. Bake for 25 minutes or until very brown. Cut into 4 wedges. Top with fruit, honey, nuts, confectioners' sugar and/or maple syrup. Yield: 4 servings.

SMASHED EGG SANDWICH

1 egg

Salt and pepper to taste

2 slices toast

BREAK the egg into a skillet. Season with salt and pepper. Fry to desired degree of doneness. Place the egg in a bowl and stir with a fork. Spread on 1 piece of toast. Top with the remaining toast. Smash together.
Yield: 1 serving.

"THE ARCHITECTURAL PROGRAM HAS TAUGHT THIS TOWN TO DREAM. WE AREN'T TIED TO THE IDEA THAT EVERYTHING HAS TO BE DONE THE TRADITIONAL WAY."

—CAROLE GOSHORN, COLUMBUS EAST HIGH SCHOOL CHEMISTRY TEACHER, 1986

BREAKFAST and BREADS

CHEF GREGORY'S OMELETTES

12 eggs

$1/2$ teaspoon Tabasco sauce

1 tablespoon milk or water

Salt and freshly ground pepper to taste

$1/2$ cup butter

$1/2$ cup olive oil

WHISK the eggs, Tabasco sauce, milk, salt and pepper in a bowl. Let the mixture come to room temperature or warm briefly in the microwave. Heat the butter and olive oil in a saucepan over low heat and keep warm. Prepare each omelette individually. Ladle $1/4$ cup of the butter mixture into a heated omelette pan. Add $1/4$ of the egg mixture when the butter mixture begins to sizzle slightly. Cook until the omelette is fluffy and sets up, stirring constantly. Add Ratatouille Filling or other fillings of choice while the omelette is still soft and moist. Fold the omelette over the filling as you slide the omelette from the pan onto the serving plate. Yield: 4 servings.

JAMES E. GREGORY MOVED TO COLUMBUS FROM CINCINNATI TO BECOME EXECUTIVE CHEF AT CUMMINS ENGINE CO. AND IRWIN MANAGEMENT CO. IN 1972. HE WAS ONE OF THE ORGANIZERS AND THE CHIEF INSPIRATION BEHIND THE HARRISON TOWNSHIP VOLUNTEER FIREMEN'S BRUNCH HELD EACH SEPTEMBER. THIS FUND-RAISER, ORGANIZED IN THE 1970'S, HAS RAISED THOUSANDS OF DOLLARS FOR EQUIPMENT WHILE SERVING THOUSANDS OF OMELETTES AND CONTINUES TODAY.

CHEF GREGORY'S RATATOUILLE FILLING

1/4 cup olive oil

1 medium onion, chopped

1 unpeeled medium eggplant, chopped

4 to 5 small zucchini, chopped

2 cups peeled seeded chopped tomatoes

1 green bell pepper, chopped

1 cup chopped celery

1/2 cup chopped fresh parsley

Jim's Four Friends

1/2 cup red wine vinegar

Salt and freshly ground pepper to taste

1 or 2 bay leaves

1 teaspoon chopped fresh thyme

1 tablespoon chopped fresh sweet basil

1/2 cup chopped fresh parsley

Olive oil

Paprika to taste

HEAT 1/4 cup olive oil in a large heavy skillet. Add the onion. Sauté until translucent. Add the eggplant. Cook for 5 minutes. Add the zucchini, tomatoes, green pepper, celery, 1/2 cup parsley, Jim's Four Friends, vinegar, salt, pepper, bay leaves, thyme and basil. Cook for 15 to 20 minutes or until the vegetables are tender, stirring frequently with a wooden spoon. Adjust the seasonings. Remove the bay leaves. Pour the vegetable mixture into an earthenware or porcelain casserole. Top with 1/2 cup parsley. Drizzle with a small amount of olive oil. Sprinkle with paprika. Chill, covered, until ready to use. Reheat at 350 degrees for 15 to 20 minutes or serve cold.

Yield: 8 servings.

JIM'S FOUR FRIENDS

1 teaspoon garlic salt

1 teaspoon MSG

1 teaspoon liquid Maggi

1 drop of Tabasco sauce

COMBINE the garlic salt, MSG, liquid Maggi and Tabasco sauce in a bowl and mix well.

BREAKFAST AND BREADS

OVERNIGHT BREAKFAST CASSEROLE

1 pound sausage

8 slices bread, crusts trimmed, cubed

1 cup shredded Swiss cheese

1 cup shredded Cheddar cheese

4 eggs

1 cup milk

$3/4$ teaspoon dry mustard

1 (10-ounce) can cream of mushroom soup

$1/2$ cup milk

1 (4-ounce) can sliced mushrooms, drained

BROWN the sausage in a skillet, stirring until crumbly; drain. Place the bread cubes in a large square baking dish sprayed with nonstick cooking spray. Add the sausage. Top with the Swiss cheese and Cheddar cheese. Beat the eggs with 1 cup milk and dry mustard in a small bowl. Pour over the cheese. Chill, covered, overnight. Mix the soup, $1/2$ cup milk and mushrooms in a bowl. Pour over the casserole. Bake at 300 degrees for $1^1/2$ hours. May substitute chopped cooked chicken for the sausage and add some cooked chopped broccoli. Yield: 6 to 8 servings.

SANDY'S SOUTHWEST BREAKFAST CASSEROLE

$1/4$ cup salsa

2 cups shredded Cheddar cheese

6 eggs, beaten

$1/2$ cup sour cream

$1/2$ cup small curd cottage cheese

4 ounces bacon, crisp-cooked, crumbled (optional)

SPREAD the salsa in a 9-inch-square baking pan. Sprinkle the Cheddar cheese over the salsa. Beat the eggs, sour cream and cottage cheese in a bowl. Pour over the Cheddar cheese. Bake at 350 degrees for 35 minutes. Remove from the oven and sprinkle the bacon over the top. Bake for 10 minutes longer or until set and light brown. Yield: 4 servings.

BAKED MIXED FRUIT

1 (16-ounce) can pineapple chunks, drained

1 (16-ounce) can sliced peaches, drained

1 (16-ounce) can sliced pears, drained

$^1/_2$ cup raisins

$^1/_2$ cup walnuts

$^1/_2$ cup packed brown sugar

1 teaspoon vanilla extract

1 (16-ounce) can apricot halves, drained

5 slices white bread, toasted, cut into $^1/_2$-inch cubes

$^1/_4$ cup packed brown sugar

$^3/_4$ cup melted margarine

MIX the pineapple, peaches, pears, raisins, walnuts, $^1/_2$ cup brown sugar and vanilla in a bowl. Spoon into a lightly greased 9x13-inch baking dish. Top with the apricot halves. Sprinkle the bread cubes over the top. Drizzle a mixture of $^1/_4$ cup brown sugar and margarine over the bread cubes. Bake at 325 degrees for 25 to 30 minutes or until heated through. Serve warm. Yield: 8 to 10 servings.

HOT CURRIED FRUIT

$^2/_3$ cup packed light brown sugar

1 tablespoon curry powder

$^1/_8$ teaspoon salt

2 tablespoons cornstarch

1 can pears

1 can apricots

1 can sliced peaches

1 can pineapple chunks

$^1/_3$ cup (about) butter or margarine

MIX the brown sugar, curry powder, salt and cornstarch together. Drain all the fruit, reserving $^1/_2$ cup juice from each can. Place half the fruit in a 9x13-inch baking dish. Top with half the brown sugar mixture. Dot with half the butter. Repeat with the remaining fruit, brown sugar mixture and butter. Pour the fruit juice over the top. Bake at 350 degrees for 40 minutes. Yield: 8 servings.

49

BREAKFAST AND BREADS

AMARETTO DIP

8 ounces cream cheese or low-fat cream cheese, softened

1 cup sugar

2 tablespoons lemon juice

$^1/_4$ cup amaretto or other liqueur, or to taste

COMBINE the cream cheese, sugar, lemon juice and amaretto in a bowl and mix well. Chill for 3 hours or longer. Serve with sliced fresh fruit. Yield: 2 to $2^1/_4$ cups.

CRANBERRY BRUNCH SQUARES

$1^1/_2$ cups sugar

2 eggs

$^3/_4$ cup melted unsalted butter, cooled

1 teaspoon almond extract

$1^1/_2$ cups flour

2 cups fresh cranberries

$^1/_2$ cup chopped pecans or almonds

BEAT the sugar and eggs in a mixer bowl for 2 minutes or until thick. Beat in the butter and flavoring. Add the flour and mix well; the batter will be thick. Add the cranberries and pecans. Pour into a greased 9-inch-square baking pan. Bake at 350 degrees for 1 hour. Let cool. Cover tightly until serving time. Cut into $1^1/_2$-inch squares. May substitute frozen Indian Trail cranberry orange relish for the cranberries. Yield: 12 servings.

IN 1900 THE EXACT POPULATION CENTER OF THE UNITED STATES WAS AT HENRY MARR'S BARN DOOR IN ROCKCREEK TOWNSHIP, WHICH IS SOUTHEAST OF COLUMBUS.

SOUPS AND SALADS

SOUPS AND SALADS

CONTENTS

OTTER CREEK CLUBHOUSE AND
GOLF COURSE, 1964. CLUBHOUSE
DESIGNED BY HARRY WEESE;
27-HOLE CHAMPIONSHIP
GOLF COURSE DESIGNED BY
ROBERT TRENT JONES AND HIS
SON REES JONES.

CREAMED AVOCADO SOUP

2 bunches green onions, finely chopped

2 tablespoons butter

1 tablespoon curry powder

1 tablespoon chopped fresh cilantro

2 medium avocados, peeled, chopped

10 cups chicken broth

$^1/_2$ cup plain yogurt

$^1/_2$ teaspoon salt

Grated peel and juice of 1 lemon

SAUTE the green onions in the butter in a skillet until tender. Add the curry powder and cilantro. Purée the green onion mixture, avocados, 1 cup of the chicken broth, yogurt, salt, lemon peel and lemon juice in a blender or food processor. Combine with the remaining 9 cups chicken broth in a large tureen or bowl. Chill until thickened. Garnish each serving with chopped cilantro and a dollop of sour cream. Serve with tortilla chips.
Yield: 8 servings.

NO-BRAINER BEEF STEW

$1^1/_2$ pounds stew beef

4 ounces fresh mushrooms, sliced

$^1/_4$ cup coarsely chopped shallots or onions

1 clove of garlic, minced

$^3/_4$ cup beef broth

$^2/_3$ cup sweet vermouth

$^1/_8$ teaspoon salt, or to taste

$^1/_2$ teaspoon cracked pepper

$1^1/_4$ tablespoons (or more) cornstarch

$^1/_4$ cup milk or skim milk

PLACE the beef in a baking dish. Stir in the mushrooms, shallots and garlic gently. Add $^1/_2$ cup of the beef broth and $^1/_2$ cup of the vermouth, stirring to mix. Bake, partially covered, for $2^1/_2$ hours, stirring occasionally. Pour the stew into a saucepan. Season with salt and pepper. Stir the cornstarch into the remaining beef broth and vermouth in a bowl. Stir into the stew. Cook until thickened. Remove from the heat and stir in the milk.
Yield: 4 to 6 servings.

PANCOTTO "BREAD" SOUP

This was one of the all-time soup favorites at Lemleys' Bistro in Columbus, Indiana.

1 cup fruity olive oil

1 large onion, finely chopped

2 to 3 cloves of garlic, minced

1 bay leaf

12 slices Italian bread with crusts, cubed

1 pound ripe Indiana tomatoes, peeled, seeded, chopped, or 1 (14-ounce) can chopped Italian tomatoes

1/2 cup chopped fresh parsley

1/2 cup chopped fresh basil

Salt and freshly ground pepper to taste

3 quarts beef stock or chicken stock

Splash of dry white wine or dry Italian vermouth

1/2 cup grated Parmesan cheese

HEAT the olive oil in a large soup kettle. Add the onion, garlic and bay leaf. Cook until translucent but not brown. Toss in the bread cubes. Sauté for 3 to 5 minutes or until light brown. Add the tomatoes. Simmer for 5 minutes. Stir in the parsley and basil. Season with salt and pepper. Add the beef stock and wine. Simmer for 10 minutes. Remove from the heat. Stir in the cheese, mixing well. Remove and discard the bay leaf. Ladle the soup into heated soup bowls. Garnish with chopped tomatoes, a small amount of olive oil, a small amount of grated Parmesan cheese and sprigs of fresh basil; or garnish with toasted pine nuts. Yield: 6 to 8 servings.

UKRAINIAN BORSCHT

3 pounds stew beef

3 quarts cold water

1 medium onion, chopped

1 bay leaf

1 parsley root, chopped

2 teaspoons salt

3 medium beets, peeled, julienned

Salt and pepper to taste

$1/2$ cup tomato sauce

1 tablespoon wine vinegar

2 large carrots, sliced

4 medium potatoes, peeled, cut into large chunks

1 small head cabbage, shredded

3 slices bacon, chopped

1 large onion, chopped

Sour cream

COMBINE the beef and cold water in a large stockpot. Add the medium onion, bay leaf, parsley root and 2 teaspoons salt. Bring to a boil; reduce the heat. Simmer until the beef is tender. Remove the beef. Skim the surface of the stock. Strain the stock, reserving $1/2$ cup. Reheat remaining stock with the beef and keep warm. Combine the beets, salt and pepper to taste, tomato sauce, vinegar and reserved stock in a saucepan. Cook, covered, over low heat until the beets are tender; keep warm. Add the carrots to the beef mixture in the stockpot. Cook over medium heat for 10 minutes. Add the potatoes and cabbage. Cook until the carrots and cabbage are tender. Add the beet mixture. Sauté the bacon and large onion in a skillet; drain. Add to the soup. Bring to a boil. Remove from the heat. Let stand for 15 to 20 minutes or until serving temperature. Remove and discard the bay leaf. Ladle the soup into bowls. Top each serving with a dollop of sour cream. For a lighter version, use low-sodium beef bouillon, omit the bacon and large onion and use low-fat sour cream. Yield: 8 servings.

HUNGARIAN GOULASH

2 tablespoons vegetable oil

4 pounds stew beef, cut into
$^1/_2$-inch pieces

2 cups chopped onions

$^1/_4$ cup flour

4 cups beef broth

2 cups peeled seeded chopped tomatoes,
or 1 (8-ounce) can chopped tomatoes

$^1/_2$ cup (or more) dry red wine (optional)

$^1/_4$ cup chopped parsley

2 tablespoons paprika, or mixed
sweet Hungarian paprika and
hot Hungarian paprika

$1^1/_2$ teaspoons marjoram

$1^1/_2$ teaspoons thyme

1 teaspoon salt, or to taste

$^1/_8$ teaspoon pepper

$^1/_2$ teaspoon caraway seeds

Grated peel of 1 lemon

$^3/_4$ cup sour cream

HEAT the oil in a Dutch oven or stockpot. Add the beef. Brown on all sides. Add the onions. Sauté until the onions are tender. Add the flour, stirring until smooth. Add the beef broth, tomatoes, wine, parsley, paprika, marjoram, thyme, salt, pepper, caraway seeds and lemon peel. Simmer, covered, for 2 to 3 hours or until the beef is tender, stirring occasionally. Ladle into bowls. Top each serving with a dollop of sour cream. Serve with spaetzle (egg noodles). Recipe may be doubled or tripled and cooked in 2 stockpots. Yield: 6 to 8 servings.

CREOLE STEW

1$^1/_2$ tablespoons vegetable oil

$^3/_4$ cup finely chopped yellow onions

$^1/_4$ cup finely chopped celery

$^1/_2$ cup finely chopped green bell pepper

2 cups fresh corn kernels

1$^1/_2$ cups thinly sliced okra

2 tablespoons minced garlic

2 bay leaves

1$^1/_2$ teaspoons dried thyme

$^1/_4$ cup butter

$^1/_2$ cup flour

1 cup chopped fresh tomatoes

4 cups chicken stock

2 cups whipping cream

1 pound crab meat, flaked

Salt, black pepper and cayenne to taste

HEAT the oil in a large stockpot. Add the onions. Cook until translucent. Add the next 7 ingredients. Cook over medium heat until the green pepper and celery are tender. Add the butter, stirring until melted. Sprinkle with the flour. Cook for 4 minutes, stirring constantly to prevent sticking. Add the tomatoes and chicken stock, stirring constantly to prevent lumps. Simmer for 5 minutes. Add the whipping cream. Simmer for 5 minutes. Add the crab meat, taking care not to break apart any lumps. Season with salt, black pepper and cayenne. Yield: 8 servings.

CHICKEN AND SPINACH SOUP

16 ounces spinach

1 pound chicken breasts

1 teaspoon cornstarch

$^1/_2$ teaspoon salt

$^1/_8$ teaspoon black pepper, or to taste

1 (49-ounce) can chicken broth

$^1/_2$ to 1 teaspoon ground ginger

1 teaspoon Beau Monde seasoning

$^1/_4$ teaspoon white pepper

WASH the spinach thoroughly and drain on paper towels. Tear into bite-size pieces. Cut the chicken crosswise into $^1/_8$-inch slices. Toss with the cornstarch, salt and black pepper in a shallow dish. Bring the chicken broth and ginger to a boil in a 5-quart saucepan. Stir in the chicken. Return to a boil. Stir in the spinach, Beau Monde seasoning and white pepper. Return to a boil; reduce the heat. Simmer, covered, for 2 minutes or until the chicken is cooked through and the spinach is tender. Yield: 6 servings.

SOUPS AND SALADS

AUNT TONI'S GAZPACHO

6 large tomatoes, peeled, seeded, finely chopped, or 2 (28-ounce) cans chopped tomatoes

2 cucumbers, seeded, finely chopped

$1/2$ cup chopped red or green bell pepper

$1/2$ cup chopped onion

2 cups vegetable juice cocktail

$1/3$ cup olive oil

3 tablespoons fresh, frozen or bottled lemon juice

Garlic salt and pepper to taste

$1/8$ to $1/4$ teaspoon Tabasco sauce, or to taste

COMBINE the tomatoes, cucumbers, red pepper and onion in a large bowl. Pour the vegetable juice cocktail, olive oil and lemon juice over the top and mix well. Season with garlic salt, pepper and Tabasco sauce and mix well. Chill for 4 hours or longer. Ladle into bowls. Garnish each serving with chopped parsley. Yield: 6 servings.

HOT AND SPICY CHILI

A favorite at the Legends of Otter Creek Golf Course

2 pounds ground beef

1 medium onion, chopped

2 (15-ounce) cans tomato sauce

2 (16-ounce) cans hot chili beans

$1^1/2$ cups water

$1/4$ cup chili powder

$1/4$ cup sugar

$1/2$ teaspoon Tabasco sauce

$1/4$ teaspoon garlic

$1/2$ teaspoon black pepper

1 teaspoon ground red pepper, or to taste

Salt and seasoned salt to taste

4 ounces spaghetti or macaroni, cooked

BROWN the ground beef with the onion in a large stockpot, stirring until the ground beef is crumbly; drain. Combine the ground beef mixture, tomato sauce, beans, water, chili powder, sugar, Tabasco sauce, garlic, black pepper, red pepper, salt and seasoned salt in the stockpot. Bring to a boil, stirring frequently. Simmer for 1 hour, stirring occasionally. Stir in the pasta.

Yield: 6 to 8 servings.

LENTIL SOUP

This is Edna Thayer's wonderful recipe, which appeared in THE REPUBLIC newspaper in November 1975.

    1 pound kielbasa, light kielbasa or
    turkey sausage

    2 quarts chicken broth

    2 cups lentils, rinsed, drained

    1 teaspoon liquid smoke

    1 large onion, chopped

    3 carrots, chopped

    2 cloves of garlic, crushed

    3 tablespoons olive oil

    1 quart canned tomatoes, chopped

    1 teaspoon thyme

    Freshly ground pepper to taste

    Chopped parsley to taste

    2 tablespoons red wine vinegar

CUT the sausage into halves lengthwise; cut into small slices. Simmer in water to cover in a saucepan over medium heat to remove excess fat; drain and pat dry. Combine the chicken broth, lentils and liquid smoke in a large stockpot. Simmer for 1 hour or until the lentils are tender. Purée 1 cup of the lentils with some of the broth in a blender; return to the soup. Cook the onion, carrots and garlic in the olive oil in a skillet until the onion is golden brown. Add to the soup. Add the tomatoes, sausage, thyme and pepper. Cook for 1 hour. Stir in the parsley and vinegar or ladle into bowls and top each serving with parsley and 1 teaspoon vinegar. Serve with homemade bread. To prepare the sausage 1 day ahead, simmer in the chicken broth for 1 hour. Chill separately overnight. Skim the chicken broth before combining with the lentils. Yield: 6 servings.

SOUPS AND SALADS

PRIZEWINNER CHILI

12 ounces Italian link sausage, cut into $^1/_2$-inch pieces

12 ounces ground beef

1 large onion, chopped

1 large green bell pepper, chopped

1 jalapeño, chopped

8 plum tomatoes, chopped

1 cup beef broth

$^1/_2$ cup Worcestershire sauce

1 can garbanzo beans, drained

1 can kidney beans, drained

1 can pinto beans, drained

1 teaspoon garlic powder

6 slices bacon, crisp-cooked, crumbled

BROWN the sausage and ground beef in a skillet, stirring frequently; drain. Brown the onion and green pepper in the skillet. Combine the sausage mixture, onion mixture, and next 8 ingredients in a large stockpot. Simmer for 2 hours. Ladle into bowls. Sprinkle with the bacon. Yield: 8 servings.

BAKED CHICKEN SALAD

3 cups chopped cooked chicken

1 tablespoon minced onion

1 cup chopped celery

1 (8-ounce) can water chestnuts, drained

1 teaspoon salt

1 teaspoon pepper

2 tablespoons lemon juice

1 hard-cooked egg, chopped (optional)

1 cup mayonnaise

1 (2-ounce) jar pimento, drained, chopped

$^1/_2$ cup slivered almonds

Shredded Cheddar cheese

$^1/_2$ cup French-fried onions, crushed

COMBINE the chicken, minced onion, celery, water chestnuts, salt, pepper, lemon juice, egg, mayonnaise, pimento and almonds in a bowl and mix well. Spoon into a greased 3-quart casserole. Cover with cheese and French-fried onions. Bake, covered, at 350 degrees for 35 to 40 minutes or until heated through. Yield: 4 to 6 servings.

CHUTNEY CHICKEN SALAD

5 cups chopped cooked chicken

1 small can water chestnuts, drained

1 small can pineapple tidbits, drained

1 cup chopped celery

$1/2$ cup chopped green onions

$1/4$ cup chutney

1 cup sour cream

1 cup light mayonnaise

1 teaspoon curry powder

MIX the chicken, water chestnuts, pineapple, celery and green onions in a large bowl. Combine the chutney, sour cream, mayonnaise and curry powder in a small bowl and mix well. Toss with the chicken mixture. May top with Chinese noodles.
Yield: 8 to 10 servings.

PERFECT PASTA SALAD

1 (16-ounce) package pasta or tri-colored pasta

1 (16-ounce) bottle Italian salad dressing

1 envelope ranch salad dressing mix

1 cup chopped purple onion

1 (16-ounce) package frozen Oriental stir-fry vegetables, thawed

2 pounds shrimp, cooked, peeled, cut into bite-size pieces

COOK the pasta using the package directions; drain. Combine the salad dressing and salad dressing mix in a small bowl or tightly sealed jar and mix well. Layer the onion and stir-fry vegetables in a large bowl. Add the warm pasta. Stir in the salad dressing mixture, tossing to coat. Add the shrimp and mix well. Chill, covered, for several hours to overnight. May add additional salad dressing if too dry.
Yield: 10 to 12 servings.

AROUND 1915, BEFORE BUILDING HIS FRIED CHICKEN EMPIRE, HARLAND SANDERS SERVED AS SECRETARY OF THE COLUMBUS CHAMBER OF COMMERCE. HE LAUNCHED A COLUMBUS COMPANY THAT MANUFACTURED CARBIDE LAMPS. THE COMPANY WENT BROKE, SANDERS MOVED TO KENTUCKY, AND THE REST IS HISTORY.

SOUPS AND SALADS

BENUENUTI'S SALAD OF BABY GREEN BEANS

16 ounces French-style green beans

Salt to taste

24 ounces white mushrooms, julienned

Benvenuti's Dressing

4 boneless duck breasts

4 ounces foie gras

16 crayfish

BLANCH the green beans in boiling salted water in a saucepan for 30 seconds. Place in ice water to keep the color and stop the cooking. Marinate the green beans and mushrooms in Benvenuti's Dressing. Sear the duck to medium in a skillet. Slice the duck very thinly. Sear the foie gras in a very hot pan. Poach the crayfish in boiling salted water in a saucepan for 45 seconds. Remove from the water and place under ice until chilled. Detach the crayfish heads and crack the shells to remove the lean tails. Arrange the green beans, mushrooms, duck, foie gras and crayfish on serving plates. Sprinkle with Benvenuti's Dressing. Yield: 8 servings.

BENUENUTI'S DRESSING

4 cups extra-virgin olive oil

1$\frac{1}{2}$ cups red wine vinegar

1 teaspoon salt

1$\frac{1}{2}$ teaspoons pepper

COMBINE the olive oil, vinegar, salt and pepper in a bowl or tightly covered jar and mix well.

PACIFIC RIM GRILLED PORK SALAD

1/4 cup dry sherry

1/4 cup soy sauce

4 teaspoons grated gingerroot

3 cloves of garlic, minced

1/3 cup water

1 1/2 pounds boneless pork loin

1/4 cup hoisin sauce

2 tablespoons brown sugar

2 tablespoons rice vinegar

1 tablespoon salad oil

1 teaspoon toasted sesame oil

8 cups torn spinach

4 cups torn Boston lettuce

6 thin slices red onion, separated into rings

1 tablespoon toasted sesame seeds

3 cups sliced pitted plums

FOR the marinade, mix the sherry, soy sauce, gingerroot, garlic and water in a large bowl. Remove and set aside 2 tablespoons of the mixture. Add the pork to the marinade. Marinate, covered, in the refrigerator for 1 hour or longer. Drain the pork, discarding the excess marinade. Grill the pork over medium-hot coals for 10 to 12 minutes or until cooked through. For the dressing, mix the reserved marinade, hoisin sauce, brown sugar, vinegar and salad oil in a saucepan. Bring to a boil. Stir in the sesame oil. Remove from the heat. Slice the pork into bite-size strips. Combine the pork, spinach, lettuce, onion and sesame seeds in a large salad bowl. Pour the hot dressing over the mixture and toss to coat. Arrange on salad plates. Arrange the plums around the edges. Yield: 6 servings.

SOUPS AND SALADS

APPLE STRAWBERRY SPINACH SALAD

1 pound spinach, rinsed, drained

2 Granny Smith apples, cubed

1 cup sliced strawberries

$^1/_2$ cup bean sprouts

4 ounces bacon, crisp-cooked, crumbled

Tangy Vinaigrette

LAYER the spinach, apples, strawberries and bean sprouts in a large salad bowl. Top with the bacon. Chill thoroughly. Add Tangy Vinaigrette at serving time. Yield: 12 servings.

TANGY VINAIGRETTE

$^3/_4$ cup vegetable oil

$^1/_3$ cup white vinegar

$^1/_2$ cup sugar

1 small onion, grated

2 teaspoons Worcestershire sauce

1 teaspoon salt

COMBINE the oil, vinegar, sugar, onion, Worcestershire sauce and salt in a bowl or tightly covered jar and mix well. Chill thoroughly.

CLESSIE CUMMINS, A SELF-TAUGHT MECHANIC AND CHAUFFEUR FOR BANKER W. G. IRWIN, HAD IDEAS FOR IMPROVING THE DIESEL ENGINE. IRWIN LIKED TO SUPPORT AMBITIOUS YOUNG MEN AND PROVIDED FINANCING TO CUMMINS. THE CUMMINS ENGINE COMPANY, FOUNDED IN 1919, WENT ON TO POWER THE FIRST DIESEL CAR AND HAS GROWN INTO THE WORLD'S LARGEST BUILDER OF DIESEL ENGINES OF 200 HORSEPOWER AND ABOVE.

DOUBLE APPLE SALAD

1 large Golden Delicious apple, cubed

1 large Red Delicious apple, cubed

1 teaspoon lemon juice

1 (20-ounce) can pineapple chunks, drained

2 tablespoons thinly sliced celery

1 cup miniature marshmallows

$^2/_3$ cup flaked coconut

$^1/_2$ cup chopped walnuts

$^1/_4$ cup raisins

$^1/_4$ cup mayonnaise

TOSS the apples with the lemon juice in a large bowl. Add the pineapple, celery, marshmallows, coconut, walnuts, raisins and mayonnaise and mix well. Chill, covered, for 1 hour or longer. Serve with chicken or turkey. Yield: 6 to 8 servings.

AVOCADOS AND PINK GRAPEFRUIT

2 pink grapefruit, peeled, divided into segments

2 large ripe avocados, peeled, thinly sliced lengthwise

Garlic Dijon Dressing

ARRANGE the grapefruit and avocados on a large round serving dish. Pour Garlic Dijon Dressing over the top. Serve immediately. Yield: 4 to 6 servings.

GARLIC DIJON DRESSING

1 teaspoon sugar

1 teaspoon Dijon mustard

1 large clove of garlic, minced

$^1/_4$ cup fresh grapefruit juice

$^1/_3$ cup olive oil

Salt and freshly ground pepper to taste

MIX the sugar, Dijon mustard and garlic in a small bowl. Pour over the grapefruit juice in a large bowl and mix well. Whisk in the oil gradually. Season with salt and pepper.

SOUPS AND SALADS

CRANBERRY SALAD

1 (14-ounce) can sweetened
condensed milk

$1/4$ cup lemon juice

1 (20-ounce) can crushed pineapple,
drained

1 (16-ounce) can whole cranberry sauce

2 cups miniature marshmallows

$1/2$ cup chopped pecans

Red food coloring (optional)

8 ounces whipped topping

Pecan halves

MIX the condensed milk and lemon juice in a
bowl. Stir in the pineapple, cranberry sauce,
marshmallows, chopped pecans and food
coloring. Fold in the whipped topping. Spoon
into a 9x13-inch dish. Freeze for 4 hours to
overnight or until firm. Cut into squares. Top
each square with a pecan half.
Yield: 12 to 18 servings.

ORANGE SHERBET SALAD

1 (6-ounce) package orange gelatin

1 cup boiling water

1 cup orange juice

1 pint orange sherbet

1 (11-ounce) can mandarin oranges,
drained

DISSOLVE the gelatin in the boiling water in
a bowl. Add the orange juice and sherbet,
mixing until the sherbet is melted and the
mixture is smooth. Chill for 30 minutes or
until partially set. Fold in the oranges. Pour
into a mold or square pan. Chill until firm.
Yield: 6 to 8 servings.

WOODY'S SALAD

1 large package lime gelatin

12 ounces whipped topping

1 large can crushed pineapple, drained

1 large package cottage cheese

2 cups miniature marshmallows

1 cup chopped pecans or walnuts (optional)

MIX the gelatin and whipped topping in a bowl. Add the pineapple, cottage cheese, marshmallows and pecans. Pour into a serving bowl. Let stand for 5 minutes before serving. Yield: 6 to 8 servings.

BROCCOLI SALAD

1 package broccoli, chopped

4 slices bacon, crisp-cooked, crumbled

$^1/_2$ cup raisins

$^3/_4$ cup shredded Cheddar cheese

2 tablespoons minced onion

$^3/_4$ cup mayonnaise-type salad dressing

$^1/_2$ cup sunflower seed kernels

MIX the broccoli, bacon, raisins, cheese, onion and salad dressing in a bowl. Chill for 2 hours or longer. Stir well. Sprinkle with the sunflower seed kernels. Yield: 8 servings.

Q. G. NOBLITT, AN ENTERPRISING BARTHOLOMEW COUNTY NATIVE, DEVISED A DEPENDABLE TIRE PUMP. WITH FRANK SPARKS AND AL REDMOND, NOBLITT STARTED THE INDIANAPOLIS AIR PUMP COMPANY IN 1919. THE COMPANY RELOCATED TO COLUMBUS IN 1931. THEIR COMPANY ALSO PRODUCED A CAR HEATER DESIGNED BY RICHARD ARVIN AND IS NOW INTERNATIONALLY KNOWN AS ARVIN INDUSTRIES, INC.

SOUPS AND SALADS

COLESLAW

2 tablespoons lemon juice

$^1/_2$ teaspoon sugar

$^1/_2$ teaspoon salt

1 tablespoon cider vinegar

$^1/_2$ cup vegetable oil

1 clove of garlic, minced

1 medium head cabbage, shredded

MIX the lemon juice, sugar, salt and vinegar in a bowl or tightly covered jar. Add the oil and mix well. Add the garlic. Let stand to allow the flavors to blend. Mix with the cabbage in a bowl at serving time. Yield: 6 to 8 servings.

CHINESE COLESLAW

1 (3-ounce) package chicken ramen noodles

1 package coleslaw

1 bunch green onions, chopped

1 to 2 tablespoons sesame seeds

3 tablespoons vinegar

2 tablespoons sugar

2 tablespoons sesame oil

$^1/_2$ cup toasted sliced almonds

CRUSH the noodles while in the package. Pour boiling water over the noodles in a colander to soften; drain well. Mix the noodles, coleslaw, green onions and sesame seeds in a large bowl. Whisk the vinegar, sugar, sesame oil and contents of the noodle seasoning packet in a medium bowl. Add to the coleslaw mixture and mix well. Chill, covered, until serving time. Add the almonds at serving time. Best if prepared ahead to allow flavors to blend. Yield: 6 to 8 servings.

CAULIFLOWER CHEESE SALAD

1 cup mayonnaise

$^1/_4$ cup sugar

1 large head cauliflower, broken into florets, chopped

1 large green bell pepper, chopped

1 very small onion, chopped

1 pound bacon, crisp-cooked, crumbled

1 cup shredded Cheddar cheese

COMBINE the mayonnaise and sugar in a small bowl and mix well. Combine the cauliflower, green pepper, onion, bacon and cheese in a large bowl. Pour the dressing over the vegetables and toss well. Chill until serving time. Yield: 6 to 8 servings.

CORN BREAD SALAD

1 (9-ounce) package corn muffin mix

1 sweet onion, chopped

1 green bell pepper, chopped

1 can kidney beans, drained

1 large tomato, chopped

8 slices bacon, crisp-cooked, crumbled

$^3/_4$ cup mayonnaise-type salad dressing

2 tablespoons pickle juice

Shredded cheese (optional)

PREPARE and bake the corn bread using the package directions. Crumble into a 9x13-inch dish. Layer the onion, green pepper, beans, tomato and bacon over the corn bread. Spread a mixture of the salad dressing and pickle juice over the top; do not stir. Top with cheese. Yield: 12 servings.

"EVERY TIME ANY PUBLIC BUILDING IS BUILT, THAT BUILDING IS A STATEMENT TO ANYONE WHO USES IT, ANYONE WHO PASSES BY, AS TO WHAT THIS CITY THINKS ABOUT ITSELF, WHAT STANDARDS IT SETS FOR ITSELF, WHAT IT AIMS TO BE."

—J. IRWIN MILLER, SPEAKING AT PRITZKER EXHIBIT, COLUMBUS, 1994

INDIANA GARDEN SALAD

$^1/_3$ cup vegetable oil

$^1/_4$ cup vinegar

$^1/_2$ cup sugar

1 teaspoon salt

$^1/_2$ teaspoon celery salt

1 medium zucchini, chopped

1 small green bell pepper, chopped

$^1/_2$ sweet onion, chopped, or
chopped green onions

2 medium tomatoes, chopped

MIX the oil, vinegar, sugar, salt and celery salt in a large bowl. Add the zucchini, green pepper, onion and tomatoes and mix well. Marinate, covered, in the refrigerator for 1 hour or longer. Yield: 4 servings.

MAMA PAT'S WILTED LETTUCE

4 large servings torn leaf lettuce

4 green onions, sliced

$^1/_4$ cup cider vinegar

$^1/_4$ cup bacon drippings, or
2 tablespoons bacon drippings plus
2 tablespoons salad oil

2 tablespoons sugar

$^1/_2$ to $^3/_4$ teaspoon salt

Freshly ground pepper to taste

4 slices bacon, crisp-cooked, crumbled

COMBINE the lettuce and green onions in a large salad bowl. Bring the vinegar, bacon drippings, sugar, salt and pepper to a boil in a saucepan. Pour over the salad. Add the bacon and toss. Serve immediately in small bowls. Yield: 4 servings.

AUNT TOT'S ARCHITECTURALLY SUPERB POTATO SALAD

This recipe came from architect Frank Adams.

1 pint whole sweet pickles

4 hard-cooked eggs

6 large potatoes

Salt to taste

1 large onion, chopped

Chopped green bell pepper

1 tablespoon whole mustard seeds

Mayonnaise-type salad dressing

DRAIN the pickles, reserving the juice. Chop or slice the pickles and set aside. Chop the eggs, reserving some center slices for a garnish. Boil the potatoes in water to cover in a saucepan. Chill the potatoes. Peel and thinly slice the potatoes. Place 1 layer of potatoes in a serving bowl. Season with salt. Pour several tablespoons of the reserved pickle juice over the potatoes. Layer pickles, onion, green pepper, eggs and mustard seeds over the potatoes. Repeat the layers until all ingredients are used. Chill, covered, for several hours to overnight. Drain well. Stir in just enough salad dressing to coat the potatoes. Garnish with egg slices, green pepper rings and paprika. Yield: 8 servings.

FRANK ADAMS OF COLUMBUS, INDIANA, DESIGNED THE DEVELOPMENTAL SERVICES BUILDING IN 1979; HE DESIGNED THE BUILDING FOR INDIANA UNIVERSITY-PURDUE UNIVERSITY AT COLUMBUS IN 1985.

DILL POTATO SALAD

1 cup ranch salad dressing

$^{1}/_{2}$ cup sliced green onions

2 tablespoons snipped fresh dill

1 teaspoon Dijon mustard

2 hard-cooked eggs, chopped

$^{1}/_{2}$ teaspoon salt

$^{1}/_{4}$ teaspoon pepper

3 pounds red potatoes, cooked, cubed

COMBINE the salad dressing, green onions, dill, Dijon mustard, eggs, salt and pepper in a bowl and mix well. Add the potatoes and mix well. Chill, covered, for several hours.
Yield: 8 servings.

GERMAN POTATO SALAD

12 ounces bacon, cubed

$^{3}/_{4}$ cup vinegar

$^{1}/_{4}$ cup water

$^{1}/_{2}$ cup sugar

1 teaspoon salt

2 tablespoons (heaping) flour

3 green onions, sliced

$^{1}/_{2}$ large sweet onion, chopped

1 teaspoon celery seeds

8 hard-cooked eggs, chopped

6 large potatoes, peeled, cooked, sliced

COOK the bacon in a skillet until crisp. Remove the bacon and drain on paper towels. Cook the vinegar, water, sugar, salt and flour in the bacon drippings in the skillet for 2 to 3 minutes or until slightly thickened, stirring constantly. Combine the dressing, green onions, onion, celery seeds, bacon, eggs and potatoes in a bowl and mix well.
Yield: 6 to 8 servings.

GREEK RICE SALAD

This recipe came from Kitty Weese, wife of architect Harry Weese.

Cold cooked rice

Chopped green bell peppers

Sliced fresh mushrooms

Raisins

Sliced almonds

Chopped scallions

Olive oil

Salt, pepper and garlic salt

COMBINE the rice, green peppers, mushrooms, raisins, almonds and scallions in a large bowl and mix well. Mix the olive oil, salt, pepper and garlic salt in a small bowl. Add to the salad and toss well. This salad is good to take on trips as it is filling and doesn't wilt. Yield: variable.

HARRY WEESE HAS LEFT HIS MARK ON TEN COLUMBUS BUILDINGS, INCLUDING THE NORTHSIDE MIDDLE SCHOOL (1961), EASTBROOK PLAZA BRANCH OF IRWIN UNION BANK AND TRUST (1961), OTTER CREEK CLUBHOUSE (1964), FIRST BAPTIST CHURCH (1965), AND CUMMINS ENGINE COMPANY TECHNICAL CENTER (1968). WEESE WAS THE ARCHITECT FOR THE LILLIAN C. SCHMITT ELEMENTARY SCHOOL (1957), THE FIRST SCHOOL IN THE CUMMINS ENGINE FOUNDATION ARCHITECTURAL PROGRAM. LINCOLN CENTER (1958), NOW HAMILTON CENTER, WAS DESIGNED AS AN OUTDOOR ICE SKATING RINK; IN 1975 AN ADDITION ENCLOSED THE RINK FOR YEAR-ROUND USE. THE IRWIN UNION BANK AND TRUST (HOPE BRANCH, 1958) AND THE BARTHOLOMEW COUNTY HOME (1959) ADD TO HIS ACCOMPLISHMENTS IN COLUMBUS.

GARDEN RICE SALAD

This recipe took second place in salads in the 1983 REPUBLIC COOKBOOK contest.

1 (6-ounce) package long grain and wild rice mix

^{1}/$_2$ cup mayonnaise or fat-free mayonnaise

^{1}/$_2$ cup sour cream or fat-free sour cream

1 cup sliced celery

1 cup chopped tomato

^{1}/$_2$ cup chopped cucumber

^{1}/$_2$ teaspoon seasoned salt

^{1}/$_4$ teaspoon pepper

Dry roasted peanuts

COOK the rice using the package directions, omitting the butter. Let cool. Toss lightly with the mayonnaise, sour cream, celery, tomato, cucumber, seasoned salt and pepper in a bowl. Garnish with peanuts. This keeps well in the refrigerator for several days without the peanuts. Yield: 8 servings.

WILD AND LONG GRAIN RICE SALAD

1 cup mixed wild and long grain rice

1^3/$_4$ cups chicken stock

1^1/$_3$ cups water

1 cup pecan pieces

1 cup currants

Grated peel of 1 orange

1 (10-ounce) package frozen peas, thawed

^{1}/$_4$ cup vegetable oil

^{1}/$_3$ cup orange juice

1 teaspoon salt

Freshly ground pepper to taste

BRING the rice, chicken stock and water to a boil in a saucepan; reduce the heat. Simmer, covered, for 25 minutes or until most of the liquid is absorbed. Combine the rice, pecans, currants, orange peel, peas, oil, orange juice, salt and pepper in a bowl and mix well. Let stand for 2 hours. Serve at room temperature over lettuce. Yield: 8 servings.

SPINACH SALAD WITH CELERY SEED DRESSING

2 packages spinach

1 Bermuda onion, sliced

1 can mandarin oranges, drained

1 package slivered almonds, blanched

Celery Seed Dressing

TOSS the spinach, onion, oranges and almonds with Celery Seed Dressing in a large bowl. Yield: 6 to 10 servings.

CELERY SEED DRESSING

1 teaspoon celery seeds

1 teaspoon salt

1 teaspoon paprika

1 teaspoon dry mustard

$^1/_3$ cup sugar

1 teaspoon grated onion

1 cup salad oil

$^1/_3$ cup vinegar

MIX the celery seeds, salt, paprika, dry mustard and sugar in a bowl. Add the onion. Add the oil and vinegar alternately, beating well after each addition.

COLORFUL SUMMER SALAD

1 cup chopped cucumber

1 cup chopped green onions

1 cup chopped celery

1 cup chopped tomatoes

1 can whole kernel corn, drained

1 bottle Italian salad dressing

COMBINE the cucumber, green onions, celery, tomatoes and corn in a bowl and mix gently. Add the salad dressing and mix well. Chill, sealed in a plastic container, overnight. Yield: 6 to 8 servings.

75

SOUPS AND SALADS

VILLA RICA TOMATO SALAD

2 cups stewed tomatoes

1 (3-ounce) package lemon gelatin

$1/2$ cup water

$1/2$ teaspoon salt

1 tablespoon vinegar

SIMMER the tomatoes in a saucepan until warm. Add the gelatin, stirring until dissolved. Add the water, salt and vinegar and mix well. Remove to a bowl. Chill for several hours or until set. Recipe may be doubled.
Yield: 4 servings.

EASY WINTER SALAD

1 cup sour cream

1 cup mayonnaise

2 teaspoons caraway seeds

1 envelope Roquefort salad dressing mix

1 head cauliflower, sliced

1 cup sliced radishes

$1/4$ cup chopped green onions

Lettuce leaves

MIX the sour cream, mayonnaise, caraway seeds and salad dressing mix in a medium bowl. Chill thoroughly. Combine the cauliflower, radishes and green onions in a large bowl. Add the dressing and mix well. Serve over lettuce leaves. Yield: 8 servings.

"WE SHAPE OUR BUILDINGS AND AFTERWARDS OUR BUILDINGS SHAPE US." —SIR WINSTON CHURCHILL

BEST SALAD DRESSING EVER

$1/2$ teaspoon garlic powder

$1/2$ teaspoon salt

3 tablespoons vegetable oil

2 to 3 tablespoons lemon juice

$2/3$ cup cider vinegar

1 cup sugar

1 teaspoon salt

$1/2$ teaspoon Beau Monde seasoning

$2/3$ cup vegetable oil

MIX the garlic powder, $1/2$ teaspoon salt and 3 tablespoons oil in a bowl. Let stand for 1 hour. Add the lemon juice and mix well. Combine the vinegar, sugar, salt and seasoning in a jar with a tightfitting lid. Cover tightly with the lid and shake well. Add $2/3$ cup oil and mix well. Add the garlic powder mixture and mix well. Store in the refrigerator.
Yield: 8 to 10 servings.

ONION SALAD DRESSING

1 cup vegetable oil

1 cup sugar

1 teaspoon salt

1 teaspoon dry mustard

1 onion, finely chopped

$1/2$ cup vinegar

1 teaspoon celery seeds

COMBINE the oil, sugar, salt, dry mustard and onion in a food processor or blender container. Process for 15 minutes. Add the vinegar and celery seeds. Process for 2 minutes. Store in the refrigerator.
Yield: 10 to 12 servings.

RASPBERRY VINAIGRETTE

$^1/_4$ cup sugar

$^1/_4$ cup raspberry vinegar

1 tablespoon poppy seeds

1 tablespoon finely chopped onion

1 teaspoon dry mustard

$^1/_2$ teaspoon salt

$^1/_2$ cup salad oil

COMBINE the sugar, vinegar, poppy seeds, onion, dry mustard, salt and oil in a jar with a tightfitting lid. Cover with the lid and shake until the sugar is dissolved. Store, covered, in the refrigerator. Serve over mixed greens, grapefruit and oranges. Yield: 6 to 8 servings.

LOW-CALORIE THOUSAND ISLAND DRESSING

1 cup plain low-fat yogurt

3 tablespoons chili sauce

2 green onions, chopped

1 tablespoon chopped green bell pepper

1 hard-cooked egg white

COMBINE the yogurt, chili sauce, green onions, green pepper and egg white in a bowl or jar with a tightfitting lid and mix well. Yield: 6 to 8 servings.

MAIN DISHES

MAIN DISHES

CONTENTS

MAIN ENTRANCE TO CUMMINS ENGINE COMPANY CORPORATE OFFICE BUILDING, 1983, DESIGNED BY KEVIN ROCHE OF ROCHE DINKELOO AND ASSOCIATES.

"GOM" SANDWICHES

Served at all the pre-game "spreads" before football and basketball games in the 1950s, these became the favorite sandwiches for that generation's children.

2 pounds ground beef

1 large onion, chopped

1 rib celery, finely chopped

$1/2$ green bell pepper, finely chopped

2 small cans tomato sauce

4 tomato sauce cans water

$1/4$ cup Worcestershire sauce

$1/4$ cup catsup

1 teaspoon garlic salt

12 hamburger buns

BROWN the ground beef in a large skillet, stirring until crumbly; drain. Add the onion. Sauté until the onion is tender. Add the celery and green pepper. Add the tomato sauce and water and mix well. Add the Worcestershire sauce, catsup and garlic salt and mix well. Cook for 30 minutes or until thickened. Serve on the buns. Yield: 12 servings.

HAMBURGER PIE

1 pound extra-lean ground beef

1 onion, chopped

Chopped celery, chopped green bell pepper or shredded carrots (optional)

Salt and freshly ground pepper to taste

$1/8$ teaspoon chili powder or fresh oregano (optional)

1 package frozen green beans, thawed

1 (10-ounce) can tomato soup

5 medium potatoes, peeled, cooked

$1/2$ cup warm milk

1 egg, beaten

$1/2$ cup shredded Colby cheese

COOK the ground beef and onion in a large skillet until the ground beef is brown and the onion is tender, stirring frequently; drain. Add the celery, salt, pepper and chili powder. Add the green beans and soup and mix well. Spoon into a greased $1^1/2$-quart casserole. Mash the potatoes in a bowl while hot. Add the milk and egg. Season with salt and pepper. Spoon into 4 to 6 mounds over the casserole. Sprinkle with the cheese. Bake at 350 degrees for 30 minutes.
Yield: 4 to 6 servings.

MAIN DISHES

MEAT LOAF

3 pounds ground beef

2 eggs, beaten

1 bottle catsup

1 package saltines, crushed

1 medium onion, chopped

MIX the ground beef, eggs, most of the catsup, cracker crumbs and onion in a bowl. Spoon into a 9x13-inch baking pan. Cover with the remaining catsup. Bake, covered with foil, at 325 degrees for 45 to 50 minutes or until the ground beef is cooked through. Yield: 6 to 8 servings.

MYSTERY MINI LOAVES

2^1/$_2$ cups soft bread crumbs

^{1}/$_2$ cup milk

3 eggs, beaten

1 envelope onion soup mix

3 pounds lean or extra-lean ground beef

^{1}/$_2$ teaspoon salt

^{1}/$_2$ teaspoon pepper

1 (12-ounce) bottle chili sauce

1 cup water

^{1}/$_2$ cup packed brown sugar

1 (16-ounce) package shredded sauerkraut

1 (16-ounce) can cranberry sauce

SOAK the bread crumbs in the milk in a bowl. Add the eggs and soup mix. Add the ground beef, salt and pepper and mix well. Shape into small loaves or balls. Place in a 9x13-inch glass baking dish. Combine the chili sauce, water, brown sugar, sauerkraut and cranberry sauce in a saucepan. Simmer for 5 minutes. Pour over the loaves. Bake at 350 degrees for 1 hour and 10 minutes or until the ground beef is cooked through. Yield: 20 servings.

NOODLE BAKE

1 (16-ounce) package egg noodles

1 pound ground beef

1 (12-ounce) can tomato sauce

2 cups ricotta cheese

11 ounces cream cheese, softened

$^1/_2$ cup sour cream

$^2/_3$ cup minced onion

2 tablespoons minced bell pepper

$^1/_4$ cup grated Parmesan cheese

COOK the noodles using the package directions. Brown the ground beef in a skillet, stirring until crumbly; drain. Stir in the tomato sauce. Remove from the heat. Beat the ricotta cheese, cream cheese, sour cream, onion and bell pepper in a mixer bowl. Drain the noodles. Layer half the noodles, all the cream cheese mixture, remaining noodles and all the ground beef mixture in a 9x13-inch baking dish. Top with the Parmesan cheese. Bake at 350 degrees for 30 minutes. Yield: 6 to 8 servings.

ITALIAN SPAGHETTI

1 pound ground beef

$^1/_2$ cup chopped onion

1 (15-ounce) can tomato sauce

1 (6-ounce) can tomato paste

1 teaspoon chili powder

$^1/_2$ teaspoon parsley flakes

1 bay leaf

Garlic powder to taste

1 (16-ounce) package spaghetti, cooked, drained

BROWN the ground beef with the onion in a skillet, stirring frequently; drain. Add the tomato sauce and tomato paste and mix well. Add the chili powder, parsley flakes, bay leaf and garlic powder. Simmer for 30 minutes. Serve over the spaghetti. Yield: 4 servings.

MAIN DISHES

GRILLED FLANK STEAK

$^1/_4$ cup low-sodium soy sauce

3 tablespoons hoisin sauce

1 tablespoon dry sherry

2 cloves of garlic, cut into halves

2 teaspoons grated fresh ginger

1 teaspoon brown sugar

1 flank steak

MIX the soy sauce, hoisin sauce, sherry, garlic, ginger and brown sugar in a shallow pan. Add the steak. Marinate, covered with plastic wrap, in the refrigerator for 48 hours or longer, turning occasionally. Remove the steak from the marinade, discarding excess marinade. Grill over hot coals to desired degree of doneness. Cut crossgrain diagonally into thin slices. Serve with grilled vegetables and herbed new potatoes. The marinade may be used for pork loin, chicken or other meats; marinate in the refrigerator for 2 hours to overnight. Yield: 4 servings.

BEEF BURGUNDY

2 large onions, chopped

$^1/_4$ cup bacon drippings

3 pounds lean beef, trimmed, cut into 1-inch cubes

3 tablespoons flour

Salt and pepper to taste

2 teaspoons fresh marjoram, or 1 teaspoon dried

3 beef bouillon cubes

2 cups boiling water

2 cups burgundy

1 pound fresh mushrooms, sliced

SAUTE the onions in the bacon drippings in a skillet. Remove the onions with a slotted spoon. Add the beef to the skillet. Cook over medium heat until brown on all sides, adding more bacon drippings if needed. Sprinkle the flour over the beef. Add the onions, salt, pepper and marjoram and mix well. Dissolve the bouillon cubes in the boiling water and add to the beef mixture. Add the wine. Spoon into a heavy casserole. Bake at 300 degrees for 4 hours, adding a mixture of 1 cup bouillon and $^1/_2$ cup wine if needed. Add the mushrooms during the last 45 minutes baking time. Serve with French bread for dipping in the sauce. Yield: 8 to 10 servings.

GOULASH WITH SAUERKRAUT

2 pounds veal or beef, cut into
1¹/₂-inch cubes

¹/₄ cup suet or butter

1¹/₂ cups sliced onions

1 clove of garlic, chopped

1 teaspoon salt

¹/₄ teaspoon pepper

1 cup chopped fresh or canned tomatoes

1 cup sour cream

2 teaspoons paprika

2 teaspoons caraway seeds

2 cups sauerkraut, rinsed, drained, heated

2 to 3 tablespoons chopped parsley
(optional)

SAUTE the veal in hot suet in a skillet until light brown. Add the onions. Cook for 5 minutes. Add the garlic, salt, pepper, tomatoes and just enough water to cover the mixture. Cook over medium heat for 45 to 60 minutes or until the veal is tender and the sauce is greatly reduced, stirring frequently. Add the sour cream, paprika and caraway seeds. Simmer for 30 minutes. Alternate layers of the goulash and sauerkraut in a warm serving dish until all ingredients are used. Sprinkle with parsley. Yield: 8 to 10 servings.

STIR-FRIED GINGERED BEEF

1 pound flank steak

¹/₃ cup water

¹/₄ cup sherry

2 tablespoons soy sauce

2 tablespoons peanut oil

1 large clove of garlic, minced

1 teaspoon shredded gingerroot

3 cups sliced radishes

1 cup diagonally sliced green onions

1 (10-ounce) can golden mushroom soup

3 to 4 servings hot cooked rice

FREEZE the steak for 1 hour for easier slicing. Cut crossgrain diagonally into thin slices. Mix the water, sherry and soy sauce in a bowl. Add the steak. Marinate for 1 hour. Heat the oil in an electric wok or 10-inch skillet at medium heat for 2 minutes. Add the steak, marinade, garlic and ginger. Cook for 5 minutes, stirring constantly. Push the mixture up the side of the wok. Add the radishes, green onions and soup. Cook for 3 minutes, stirring constantly. Serve over the rice. Yield: 3 to 4 servings.

MAIN DISHES

PUCHERO

This recipe came from architect Cesar Pelli.

2 pounds beef short ribs

8 cups cold water

8 marrow bones

2 sweet potatoes, peeled, chopped

3 potatoes, peeled, chopped

1 onion, sliced

1 piece yellow squash (about $^1/_2$ pound)

4 carrots, sliced

1 can garbanzo beans (optional)

COMBINE the beef, water and marrow bones in a large saucepan. Boil for 15 minutes. Skim the surface. Add the sweet potatoes, potatoes, onion, squash, carrots and beans and mix well. Add additional water if needed. Cook, loosely covered, until the vegetables are tender. Arrange the vegetables and beef in a serving dish. Reserve the cooking liquid for making soup. Vegetables may be varied seasonally. Yield: 8 servings.

IN 1973 CESAR PELLI DESIGNED THE COMMONS AND COURTHOUSE CENTER. ALL UNDER COVER AND ENCLOSED WITH BROWN GLASS, THIS PUBLIC SPACE INCLUDES EXHIBIT HALLS, STAGE, PLAYGROUND, MOVIE THEATERS, RESTAURANTS, MEETING ROOMS AND RETAIL SHOPS. THE COMMONS ALSO IS HEADQUARTERS FOR THE COLUMBUS AREA ARTS COUNCIL, WHICH SPONSORS A VARIETY OF CULTURAL ACTIVITIES FOR THE COMMUNITY.

ROAST BEEF WITH FRESH GARLIC AND SEASONING SALT

1 (7-pound) beef rib roast, cut from the small end, approximately 3 ribs

2 tablespoons vegetable oil

Seasoning Salt

HAVE the butcher cut off the rib bones and tie them back on (oven-ready). Dry the roast with paper towels. Rub all sides with oil. Rub Seasoning Salt over all sides and the top. Place in a shallow pan. Chill, covered loosely with foil, overnight. Remove from the refrigerator and let stand for 1 hour. Roast on the lowest oven rack at 450 degrees for 30 minutes or until seared. Reduce the oven temperature to 325 degrees. Roast for $1^{1}/_{4}$ hours or to desired degree of doneness. Remove to a platter. Let stand for 15 minutes or longer. Slice and serve.

Yield: 10 to 12 servings.

SEASONING SALT

4 to 6 large cloves of garlic, minced

$1^{1}/_{2}$ tablespoons salt

$^{1}/_{2}$ teaspoon sweet paprika

$^{1}/_{2}$ teaspoon turmeric

$^{1}/_{2}$ teaspoon ground thyme

1 teaspoon pepper

MIX the garlic, salt, paprika, turmeric, thyme and pepper in a bowl.

MAIN DISHES

FLETA'S CHICKEN IN PUFF PASTRY

1 (17-ounce) package puff pastry

1 (4-ounce) package Alouette garlic and spice cheese, or 3 ounces cream cheese with onions and chives, softened

1¹/₂ teaspoons chopped parsley

6 boneless skinless chicken breast halves

¹/₂ teaspoon salt

¹/₈ teaspoon pepper

1 egg, beaten

1 tablespoon water

UNFOLD the pastry sheets. Roll each sheet into a 12x14-inch rectangle on a lightly floured surface. Cut 1 sheet into four 6x7-inch rectangles. Cut two 6x7-inch rectangles from the other sheet; set aside the remaining pastry. Shape the 6 small rectangles into ovals. Spread each oval with Alouette cheese. Sprinkle with the parsley. Sprinkle the chicken with the salt and pepper. Place 1 chicken piece on each pastry oval. Moisten the edges of the ovals with a small amount of water. Fold the ends over the chicken; fold the sides over. Press to seal the edges of the bundles. Place the bundles seam side down on a lightly greased baking sheet. Cut the remaining pastry into thin 12-inch strips. Braid 2 strips together; place crosswise over each bundle. Chill, covered, until needed. Mix the egg and 1 tablespoon water in a bowl. Brush over the pastry bundles. Bake on the lower oven rack at 400 degrees for 25 minutes or until the pastry is golden brown and the chicken is cooked through. Yield: 6 servings.

CHICKEN CASSEROLE

1 package refrigerated noodles

1 (10-ounce) can cream of chicken soup

$^2/_3$ cup evaporated milk

$1^1/_2$ cups shredded American cheese

Salt to taste

4 or 5 boneless skinless chicken breasts, cooked, chopped

$^3/_4$ cup chopped onion

1 cup chopped celery

1 can sliced water chestnuts

$^1/_2$ package herb-flavor stuffing mix

COOK the noodles using the package directions; drain. Combine the soup, evaporated milk, cheese and salt in a saucepan. Heat until the cheese melts, stirring occasionally. Mix the chicken, onion, celery and water chestnuts in a bowl. Layer the noodles and chicken mixture in a greased 9x13-inch casserole. Pour the cheese mixture over the top. Sprinkle with the stuffing mix. Bake at 350 degrees for 30 minutes. Yield: 6 to 8 servings.

ZESTY CHICKEN AND RICE

4 chicken breasts, cut into halves

$^1/_3$ cup bottled Italian salad dressing

$^2/_3$ cup rice

1 (16-ounce) package frozen mixed broccoli, carrots, water chestnuts and red pepper, or mixed Oriental vegetables

1 (3-ounce) can French-fried onions

$1^3/_4$ cups chicken bouillon

$^1/_2$ teaspoon Italian seasoning

ARRANGE the chicken in a single layer in an 8x12-inch baking dish. Pour the salad dressing over the chicken. Bake at 400 degrees for 20 minutes. Place the rice, mixed vegetables and half the onions around and under the chicken. Pour a mixture of the bouillon and Italian seasoning over the top. Bake at 400 degrees for 25 minutes. Top with the remaining onions. Bake for 2 to 3 minutes longer. Let stand for 5 minutes before serving. Yield: 4 servings.

MAIN DISHES

PEPPERONCINI IN PHYLLO

6 ounces hot pepper cheese, goat cheese or ricotta cheese

24 pepperoncini (pickled hot peppers)

6 ounces boneless skinless chicken breasts

12 sheets phyllo pastry

$^1/_2$ cup melted unsalted butter

48 long chive leaves, blanched

CUT the cheese into $^1/_4$-ounce pieces. Cut the tops off the peppers and remove the seeds. Cut the chicken into $^1/_4$-ounce pieces. Stuff each pepperoncini with 1 piece of chicken and 1 piece of cheese. Set aside. Brush a sheet of phyllo with melted butter. Add a second sheet and brush with butter; add a third sheet and brush with butter. Cut into thirds cross-wise; cut into halves lengthwise to form 6 portions. Place 1 pepper 1 inch from the narrow end of the pastry; roll the pastry around the pepper like a cigar. Twist the ends. Repeat with the remaining pastry, butter and peppers. Place the pastry bundles on a buttered baking sheet with sides. Bake at 375 degrees for 20 to 30 minutes or until the pastry is golden brown. Tie the twisted ends with the blanched chives. May omit chicken to serve as an appetizer. May be frozen before baking; bake without thawing.

Yield: 12 servings.

CHICKEN BREASTS WITH BLEU CHEESE AND SOUR CREAM

³/₄ tablespoon butter

8 boneless skinless chicken breasts

2 cups sour cream

4 ounces bleu cheese

1 tablespoon Worcestershire sauce

Garlic salt to taste, or 1 clove of garlic, minced

MELT the butter in a large skillet over medium heat. Add the chicken. Cook for 4 minutes per side or until brown. Remove to a 9x13-inch casserole. Mix the sour cream, cheese, Worcestershire sauce and garlic salt in a small bowl. Spoon evenly over the chicken. Bake at 350 degrees for 45 minutes or until the chicken is cooked through. Garnish with parsley. Serve over rice. Do not use light or fat-free sour cream in this recipe.
Yield: 8 servings.

CHICKEN BREASTS WITH GARLIC AND CREAM

Herb-flavor stuffing mix

4 whole boneless skinless chicken breasts, cut into halves

Salt and pepper to taste

2 eggs, beaten

¹/₂ cup butter

¹/₄ cup olive oil

8 ounces mushrooms, sliced

2 cups whipping cream

¹/₂ teaspoon salt

5 plump cloves of garlic, crushed

¹/₂ teaspoon paprika

PROCESS the stuffing mix in a food processor to the consistency of bread crumbs. Season the chicken with salt and pepper to taste. Dip in the eggs; roll in the crumbs. Sauté in the butter and oil in a skillet until golden brown. Remove to a 9x13-inch baking dish. Sauté the mushrooms in the skillet, adding additional butter if needed. Pour over the chicken. Pour a mixture of the whipping cream, ¹/₂ teaspoon salt and garlic over the chicken. Bake, covered with foil, at 350 degrees for 45 to 60 minutes or until the chicken is cooked through. Sprinkle with the paprika. Serve with rice and a green salad. Yield: 4 to 8 servings.

MAIN DISHES

ELEGANT CHICKEN AND SEAFOOD CASSEROLE

4 (8-ounce) cans artichoke hearts, drained

4 pounds crab meat or shrimp, cleaned, cooked

8 chicken breasts, cooked, chopped

3 pounds fresh mushrooms, sliced

3 tablespoons butter

1^1/$_2$ cups flour

6 cups milk

^{1}/$_2$ cup melted butter

2 tablespoons Worcestershire sauce

Salt and pepper to taste

1 cup sherry

^{1}/$_2$ cup grated Parmesan cheese

Paprika to taste

Chopped parsley

ARRANGE the artichoke hearts in a large buttered casserole. Add the crab meat and chicken. Sauté the mushrooms in 3 table-spoons butter in a large skillet; drain. Add the mushrooms to the casserole. Heat the flour, milk and melted butter in a saucepan until thick and creamy, stirring constantly. Add the Worcestershire sauce, salt, pepper and sherry and mix gently. Spoon over the mushrooms. Sprinkle with cheese. Dust with paprika and parsley. Bake at 375 degrees for 40 minutes or until the chicken is cooked through. Serve over rice. Yield: 20 servings.

CHICKEN SUISSE

3 whole chicken breasts, cut into halves, boned

6 slices Swiss cheese

^{1}/$_4$ cup white wine

1 (10-ounce) can cream of mushroom soup

Crushed garlic and onion croutons

Salt and pepper to taste

^{1}/$_4$ cup melted butter

ARRANGE the chicken in a baking dish. Cover each piece with 1 slice of cheese. Spoon a mixture of the wine and soup over the top. Cover with crouton crumbs. Season with salt and pepper. Drizzle with the butter. Bake at 350 degrees for 1 hour. Yield: 6 servings.

GREEN CHILE CHICKEN CASSEROLE

2 large chicken breasts, boiled, boned, chopped

$^1/_2$ cup chopped onion

1 (10-ounce) can cream of chicken soup

1 can chicken broth

1 small can green chiles

1 small can chopped black olives

12 small corn tortillas

1 pound Cheddar cheese, shredded

MIX the chicken, onion, soup, broth, green chiles and olives in a bowl. Cover the bottom of a 2-quart casserole with a small amount of the liquid from the mixture. Add layers of 4 tortillas, $^1/_3$ of the chicken mixture and $^1/_3$ of the cheese until all the ingredients are used. Bake at 350 degrees for 40 minutes. Garnish with sour cream and salsa. Yield: 8 servings.

LEMON THYME CHICKEN SCALOPPINE

4 boneless skinless chicken breasts

Flour

1 tablespoon butter

1 tablespoon vegetable oil

$^1/_3$ cup dry white wine or chicken broth

$^1/_4$ cup whipping cream

1 teaspoon lemon juice

$^1/_4$ teaspoon thyme leaves

Salt and pepper to taste

PLACE the chicken between sheets of waxed paper or plastic wrap. Pound evenly until the chicken is $^1/_4$ inch thick. Dust with flour, shaking to remove any excess. Cook in the butter and oil in a skillet over medium-high heat for $1^1/_2$ minutes per side or until cooked through. Remove to a warm platter. Add the wine to the pan drippings in the skillet. Boil until reduced by $^1/_2$. Add the whipping cream, lemon juice and thyme. Boil until slightly thickened. Season with salt and pepper. Pour over the chicken. Garnish with parsley and lemon wedges. Yield: 2 to 3 servings.

MAIN DISHES

POPPY SEED CHICKEN

2 sleeves butter crackers, crushed

1 cup melted margarine

2 tablespoons poppy seeds

2 (10-ounce) cans cream of chicken soup

2 cups sour cream

6 to 8 chicken breasts, cooked, boned, cut into chunks

MIX the cracker crumbs, margarine and poppy seeds in a small bowl. Mix the soup and sour cream in a medium bowl. Coat a 9x13-inch casserole with butter or vegetable cooking spray. Spread half the cracker mixture in the prepared casserole. Add layers of chicken and the soup mixture. Top with the remaining cracker mixture. Bake at 350 degrees for 1 hour. Yield: 8 servings.

PARMESAN CHICKEN WITH MARSALA

$1/4$ cup fine bread crumbs

$1/4$ cup freshly grated Parmesan cheese

$1/4$ teaspoon paprika

$1/4$ teaspoon garlic powder

$1/8$ teaspoon thyme

Freshly ground pepper to taste

1 tablespoon minced parsley

4 boneless skinless chicken breasts

$1/3$ cup water

1 tablespoon vegetable oil

$1/4$ cup melted margarine

$1/3$ cup marsala

MIX the bread crumbs, cheese, paprika, garlic powder, thyme, pepper and parsley in a paper bag. Add the chicken, shaking until coated. Pour the water into an oiled baking pan. Arrange the chicken in a single layer in the pan. Sprinkle with a mixture of the oil and margarine. Bake at 350 degrees for 20 minutes. Reduce the oven temperature to 325 degrees. Pour the wine over the chicken. Bake, covered with foil, for 15 minutes. Increase the oven temperature to 350 degrees. Bake, uncovered, for 10 to 15 minutes or until the chicken is cooked through. Cool slightly before serving. Yield: 4 servings.

RUSSIAN CHICKEN

4 chicken breasts

1 bottle Russian salad dressing

1 (12-ounce) jar apricot preserves

1 envelope onion soup mix

ARRANGE the chicken in a baking dish. Combine the salad dressing, preserves and soup mix in a saucepan. Bring to a boil. Spoon over the chicken. Bake, covered, at 325 degrees for $1^1/_2$ hours. Increase the oven temperature to 350 degrees. Bake, uncovered, for 20 to 30 minutes or until the chicken is brown and cooked through, basting occasionally. Yield: 4 servings.

EASY BAKED CURRIED CHICKEN

2 tablespoons butter or margarine

1 unpeeled apple, finely chopped

1 small onion, finely chopped

1 tablespoon curry powder

1 cup milk

1 (10-ounce) can cream of mushroom soup

1 chicken, cut up, or equivalent amount of chicken pieces

Salt and paprika to taste

MELT the butter in a small saucepan. Add the apple, onion and curry powder. Sauté until the onion is translucent. Add a mixture of the milk and soup and mix well. Arrange the chicken in a shallow baking pan. Sprinkle with salt and paprika. Pour the sauce over the chicken. Bake at 350 degrees for $1^1/_2$ hours. If using boneless chicken pieces, begin checking for doneness after 45 minutes.
Yield: 3 to 4 servings.

MAIN DISHES

FUSILLI WITH SHREDDED CHICKEN

This recipe came from architects Peter Stamberg and Paul Aferiat.

8 ounces fusilli, cooked

2 whole chicken breasts, cooked, shredded

2 cups chopped drained artichoke hearts

$1/2$ cup thinly sliced sun-dried tomatoes

Mustard Dressing

$1/2$ cup chopped fresh herbs such as basil, parsley and/or chives

COMBINE the pasta, chicken, artichoke hearts, tomatoes and Mustard Dressing in a large bowl. Stir in the herbs just before serving. Serve with spinach salad or fresh fruit and French bread. Yield: 4 servings.

MUSTARD DRESSING

$1/2$ cup Dijon mustard

$1/2$ cup boiling water

1 cup olive oil

6 tablespoons white wine vinegar

1 clove of garlic

Salt and freshly ground pepper to taste

PLACE the mustard in a food processor container. Keep the food processor running while adding the remaining ingredients in the order listed; add liquid ingredients gradually.

PETER STAMBERG AND PAUL AFERIAT HAVE BEEN COMMISSIONED TO RENOVATE AND ADD ON TO CLIFTY CREEK ELEMENTARY SCHOOL. ORIGINALLY DESIGNED BY RICHARD MEIER IN 1982, CLIFTY CREEK WAS THE SECOND RURAL SCHOOL BUILT UNDER THE CUMMINS ENGINE FOUNDATION ARCHITECTURAL PROGRAM. STAMBERG AND AFERIAT HAVE DONE TWO OTHER RENOVATIONS AND/OR ADDITIONS TO BUILDINGS ORIGINALLY DESIGNED BY MEIER. ACCORDING TO MEIER, THEY HAVE BROUGHT THEIR OWN VISION TO THESE PROJECTS RATHER THAN ATTEMPTING MINDLESS IMITATIONS. THEY WERE ABLE TO SYNTHESIZE THE OVERRIDING CONCEPTS OF THE BUILDINGS AND EXPAND AND UPDATE THEM TO SATISFY CHANGING NEEDS. CLIFTY CREEK ELEMENTARY SCHOOL IS THE SCHOOL ARCHITECTURAL STUDENTS AND ARCHITECTS MOST FREQUENTLY ASK TO VISIT.

HAWAIIAN CHICKEN

1 cup sugar

2 teaspoons salt

2 teaspoons ground ginger

Pepper to taste

2 chickens, cut up, or 32 mixed legs
and thighs

Flour

Vegetable oil

1 large can pineapple juice

2 tablespoons soy sauce

MIX the sugar, salt, ginger and pepper
together. Roll the chicken in the mixture until
coated. Place in a shallow dish. Chill, covered,
overnight. Coat the chicken with flour 3 to 4
hours before serving time. Cook in oil in a
Dutch oven or heavy ovenproof skillet over
low heat until brown; be sure to use low heat
as the chicken will burn easily. Pour a mixture
of the pineapple juice and soy sauce over the
chicken. Bake, covered, at 325 degrees for 2 to
3 hours or until the chicken is very tender and
cooked through; uncover during the last hour
of baking. Yield: 12 to 16 servings.

CHICKEN A LA KING

1 package pastry shells

$1/2$ cup chopped green bell pepper

2 tablespoons butter

1 (10-ounce) can cream of chicken soup

$1/2$ cup milk

2 cups chopped cooked chicken

$1/4$ cup chopped pimentos

BAKE the pastry shells using the package
directions. Set aside and keep warm. Cook the
green pepper in the butter in a saucepan until
tender. Add the soup, milk, chicken and
pimentos. Cook until heated through. Spoon
into the pastry shells. Yield: 6 servings.

MAIN DISHES

MANDARIN CHICKEN

This recipe took first place in main dishes in the REPUBLIC COOKBOOK contest.

1 cup barbecue sauce

1 cup orange juice

$^1/_2$ cup packed brown sugar

$^1/_4$ cup flour

$^1/_4$ cup vegetable oil

$^1/_4$ teaspoon salt

4 cups chopped cooked chicken

1 (20-ounce) can pineapple chunks, drained

$^1/_2$ cup sliced water chestnuts

1 teaspoon candied ginger (optional)

COMBINE the barbecue sauce, orange juice, brown sugar, flour, oil and salt in a saucepan. Cook over medium heat for 5 minutes or until bubbly and slightly thickened, stirring constantly. Add the chicken, pineapple, water chestnuts and ginger. Simmer, covered, over low heat for 10 minutes, stirring occasionally. Serve over hot cooked rice. May top with macadamia nuts or almonds. Yield: 6 servings.

COLUMBUS CHICKEN ENCHILADAS

1 (16-ounce) can tomatoes with green chiles

1 tablespoon chopped fresh cilantro

1 cup sour cream

2 cups shredded poached chicken

3 ounces cream cheese, softened

$^1/_4$ cup chopped onion

$^3/_4$ teaspoon salt

12 corn tortillas

2 cups shredded 4-cheese Mexican blend

PROCESS the tomatoes, cilantro and sour cream in a blender until smooth. Pour into a pie plate and set aside. Mix the chicken, cream cheese, onion and salt in a bowl and set aside. Microwave the tortillas for 30 seconds or until softened. Dip 1 tortilla at a time into the tomato mixture just until limp. Spread the tortillas with the chicken mixture; roll up. Place seam side down in a 7x12-inch baking dish. Pour the remaining tomato mixture over the top. Cover with the cheese. Bake at 350 degrees for 30 minutes or until the cheese is golden brown. Garnish with avocado slices, olive slices, sour cream and chopped cilantro. Yield: 6 servings.

COMPANY CHICKEN CASSEROLE

12 slices bread, crusts trimmed

6 cups chopped cooked chicken

8 ounces mushrooms, sliced

1 can sliced water chestnuts

1 (10-ounce) can each cream of celery soup and cream of mushroom soup

$1/2$ cup mayonnaise

1 (2-ounce) jar chopped pimento

8 ounces Cheddar cheese, shredded

1 teaspoon salt

2 cups milk

4 eggs, beaten

$1/2$ package seasoned croutons, crushed

$1/4$ cup butter or margarine

LAYER the bread, chicken, mushrooms and water chestnuts in a greased 12x20-inch baking dish. Spread with a mixture of the soups and mayonnaise. Sprinkle with the pimento and cheese. Pour a mixture of the salt, milk and eggs over the top. Chill, covered, overnight. Bake, covered, at 350 degrees for 30 minutes. Sauté the crouton crumbs in the butter in a skillet. Sprinkle over the top of the casserole. Bake for 30 minutes longer.
Yield: 10 to 12 servings.

BEST-EVER BAKED HAM

1 (8- to 10-pound) ham

1 (8-ounce) jar Dijon mustard

1 (1-pound) package brown sugar

1 (12-ounce) can Coca-Cola

PLACE the ham in a shallow baking dish. Spread with the Dijon mustard. Pack the brown sugar over the ham. Pour the Coca-Cola into the pan. Bake at 350 degrees for 10 minutes per pound. Do not baste. The sauce will be lumpy but good for dipping.
Yield: 20 to 25 servings.

MAIN DISHES

TABERNACLE HAM LOAF

This recipe first appeared in the 1932 CIRCLE COOK BOOK OF TESTED AND TRIED RECIPES, compiled and published by the Young Ladies Mission Circle of the Tabernacle Church of Christ, Columbus, Indiana. All the recipes in this 40-page cookbook are "from scratch"— no shortcuts back then!

1 pound smoked ham

1 pound lean pork

8 honey graham cracker squares, ground

2 eggs, lightly beaten

$^1/_2$ cup milk

1 teaspoon salt (optional)

$^1/_2$ teaspoon pepper

Horseradish (optional)

Whipped topping (optional)

HAVE your butcher grind the ham and pork together twice. Combine the ham mixture, cracker crumbs, eggs, milk, salt and pepper in a large bowl and mix well. Pack into a 5x9-inch loaf pan. Bake at 325 degrees for 2 hours or until slightly browned. Remove from the oven and let stand for 10 minutes. Loosen from the edges of the pan. Use 1 turner at each end of the loaf to remove the loaf to a platter. Serve with a sauce made of horseradish and whipped topping.

Yield: 8 to 10 servings.

LETTERMAN HOAGIE

In revising the 4th Street Bar menu to add pizza and baked sandwiches, we were trying to create an appealing selection. One night, David Letterman said that his favorite sandwich was this combination of ingredients. We added the sandwich to the menu, and it remains one of the most popular selections.

1 (6-inch) hoagie bun, sliced open horizontally

$^3/_4$ cup shredded mozzarella cheese

$^1/_2$ cup thinly sliced ham

6 pepperoni slices

$^1/_4$ cup bacon bits

3 tomato slices

$^1/_4$ cup chopped lettuce

2 tablespoons Italian dressing

OPEN the bun onto a baking sheet. Sprinkle each half with the cheese. Cover 1 half with the ham; cover the other with pepperoni and bacon bits. Bake at 350 degrees for 7 minutes. Arrange the tomato slices and lettuce over one half. Drizzle that half with the Italian dressing. Close the sandwich. Cut the sandwich diagonally into halves. Yield: 1 serving.

CUMMINS ENGINES, MADE IN COLUMBUS, ARE KNOWN FOR THEIR HEAVY-DUTY PERFORMANCE ON THE HIGHWAYS, BUT THEY ALSO PLAYED A PART IN RACING HISTORY. IN THE 1930 INDIANAPOLIS 500, A CUMMINS-POWERED DIESEL RACER SET A RECORD FOR COMPLETING THE RACE WITHOUT A PIT STOP—A RECORD THAT STILL STANDS TODAY.

MAIN DISHES

SPAGHETTI ALLA CARBONARA

This recipe came from Tiziana Hardy, wife of architect Hugh Hardy.

8 ounces bacon

1 tablespoon vegetable oil

1¼ pounds spaghetti

6 eggs

2 tablespoons whipping cream

Salt and freshly ground pepper to taste

4 ounces Parmesan cheese or Romano cheese, grated

CUT the bacon into ¼-inch slices, then into ¼-inch strips. Sauté in the oil in a large skillet until cooked through but not dry. Cook the spaghetti for 3 minutes less than directed on the package for al dente; drain. Combine with the bacon in the skillet. Cook until the spaghetti is al dente. Beat the eggs, whipping cream, salt and pepper in a bowl until slightly foamy. Add quickly to the skillet and toss well. Remove immediately to a warm serving dish. Top with the cheese. Yield: 4 to 6 servings.

IN 1972 HUGH HARDY OF HARDY HOLZMAN PFEIFFER ASSOCIATES OF NEW YORK CITY DESIGNED MT. HEALTHY ELEMENTARY SCHOOL. THIS SCHOOL IS THE FIRST RURAL BARTHOLOMEW COUNTY SCHOOL BUILT UNDER THE CUMMINS ENGINE FOUNDATION ARCHITECTURAL PROGRAM AND THE FIRST UNDER AN OPEN CLASSROOM TEACHING PLAN. HARDY ALSO DESIGNED THE COLUMBUS OCCUPATIONAL HEALTH ASSOCIATION BUILDING, WHICH SERVES EMPLOYEES OF MORE THAN 190 COMPANIES IN FIFTEEN STATES AND MEXICO.

JAMBALAYA PASTA

1 cup finely chopped onion

1 cup finely chopped green bell pepper

1 cup finely chopped celery

2 cloves of garlic, minced

2 tablespoons vegetable oil

1 (14-ounce) can tomatoes, chopped

1 cup chicken broth

1 (6-ounce) can tomato paste

1 teaspoon crushed dried oregano

$^1/_2$ teaspoon crushed dried basil

$^1/_2$ teaspoon crushed dried thyme

$^1/_2$ teaspoon ground red pepper, or to taste

$^1/_2$ teaspoon ground black pepper

8 ounces bow tie pasta

12 ounces large shrimp, peeled

4 cups boiling water

8 ounces spicy pork sausage or other sausage, cooked, drained

1 cup chopped cooked ham

COOK the onion, green pepper, celery and garlic in the oil in a large saucepan for 5 to 7 minutes or until tender but not brown; do not drain. Add the tomatoes, chicken broth and tomato paste. Stir in the oregano, basil, thyme, red pepper and black pepper. Simmer, covered, for 20 minutes. Cook the pasta using the package directions; drain. Drop the shrimp into the boiling water in a stockpot; reduce the heat. Simmer for 1 to 3 minutes or until the shrimp turn pink, stirring occasionally; drain. Add the sausage and ham to the tomato sauce. Cook until heated through. Combine the tomato sauce, shrimp and pasta in a large serving bowl and toss gently.

Yield: 6 to 8 servings.

IN 1929 G. L. REEVES, PRESIDENT OF THE COLUMBUS CHAMBER, MADE A RADIO ADDRESS OVER STATION WFBM IN INDIANAPOLIS. DURING THIS ADDRESS HE SAID, "WE ARE NOT ATTEMPTING TO BUILD THE LARGEST CITY AT COLUMBUS, BUT SIMPLY THE BEST."

MAIN DISHES

PORK CHOP CASSEROLE

4 to 6 pork chops

Vegetable oil

2 (10-ounce) cans cream of mushroom soup

$^3/_4$ cup sour cream

$^1/_2$ cup water

$^1/_4$ cup parsley flakes

6 to 8 large potatoes, peeled, sliced

BROWN the pork chops lightly in oil in a skillet; drain well. Mix the soup, sour cream, water and parsley flakes in a bowl. Place a small amount of the soup mixture in a greased large baking pan; reserve a small amount of the mixture for a topping. Alternate layers of the soup mixture and potatoes in the pan. Top with the pork chops. Spread with the reserved soup mixture. Bake, covered, at 350 degrees for 2 hours. May be prepared ahead and stored in the refrigerator until baking time. Yield: 4 servings.

BAKED PORK CHOPS IN VERMOUTH

This recipe came from architect John M. Johansen.

4 pork chops

Chopped garlic to taste

Salt and pepper to taste

$^1/_2$ cup dry vermouth

$^3/_4$ cup sour cream

Poppy seeds to taste

RUB the pork chops with garlic, salt and pepper. Place in a shallow casserole dish. Pour the vermouth over the pork chops. Cover with the sour cream. Sprinkle the poppy seeds over the top. Bake at 375 degrees until the pork chops are cooked through. Yield: 4 servings.

SKILLET BARBECUE PORK CHOPS

6 ($^1/_2$-inch-thick) pork chops

1 tablespoon vegetable oil

$^1/_2$ cup water

$^1/_4$ cup teriyaki sauce

$^1/_4$ cup catsup

4 teaspoons brown sugar

4 teaspoons cornstarch

$^1/_4$ cup water

BROWN the pork chops in the oil in a skillet; drain. Mix $^1/_2$ cup water, teriyaki sauce, catsup and brown sugar in a bowl. Pour over the pork chops. Simmer, covered, for 1 hour, turning the pork chops after 30 minutes. Remove the pork chops from the skillet. Dissolve the cornstarch in $^1/_4$ cup water. Stir into the skillet. Cook until thickened, stirring constantly. Return the pork chops to the skillet, turning to coat both sides with the sauce.
Yield: 6 servings.

JOHN M. JOHANSEN OF NEW CAANAN, CONNECTICUT, DESIGNED THE L. FRANCIS SMITH ELEMENTARY SCHOOL IN 1969. JOHANSEN DESIGNED SEVEN BRIGHTLY PAINTED STEEL RAMPS OR "TUBES" CONNECTING THE MULTI-LEVELS OF THE STEEL STRUCTURE.

MAIN DISHES

MARINATED ROAST PORK TENDERLOIN WITH MANGO SALSA

2 cloves of garlic, peeled, sliced

$^1/_4$ cup olive oil

Juice of 1 large lemon

$1^1/_2$ tablespoons fresh thyme, or $^1/_2$ teaspoon dried

2 teaspoons cracked pepper

2 (1-pound) pork tenderloins, trimmed

1 tablespoon olive oil

1 tablespoon unsalted butter

Coarse salt to taste

$1^1/_4$ cups brown chicken stock or beef stock

3 tablespoons unsalted butter

Mango Salsa (page 107)

MIX the garlic, $^1/_4$ cup oil, lemon juice, thyme and pepper in a small bowl. Place the tenderloins in a heavy zip-top plastic bag. Pour the marinade over the pork and seal the bag. Let stand at room temperature for 2 hours, turning frequently. Remove the pork from the bag and dry with paper towels. Discard the remaining marinade. Heat 1 tablespoon oil and 1 tablespoon butter in a large ovenproof skillet over high heat. Add the pork. Brown on all sides. Season with coarse salt. Add $^1/_4$ cup of the chicken stock. Roast at 425 degrees for 16 to 20 minutes or until cooked through, adding a small amount of the chicken stock to the pan and basting frequently with pan drippings. Remove the pork to a carving board and set aside. Degrease the pan drippings and return to the skillet with the remaining chicken stock. Cook until reduced, thickening with beurre manié if desired (see Note). Remove from the heat. Add 3 tablespoons butter, whisking until smooth. Adjust seasonings. Serve with Mango Salsa. Note: Beurre manié is made by creaming equal parts flour and butter; it may be prepared ahead and stored in the refrigerator. Yield: 6 servings.

MANGO SALSA

3 tablespoons lime juice

2 tablespoons brown sugar

2 tablespoons fish sauce

1 teaspoon Chinese chili sauce or minced jalapeños

2 tablespoons minced green onions

1 tablespoon finely minced ginger

2 small ripe mangoes, peeled, chopped

1 papaya or 4 peaches, peeled, seeded, chopped

2 tablespoons cilantro

MIX the lime juice, brown sugar, fish sauce and chili sauce in a small bowl. Mix the green onions, ginger, mangoes and papaya in a large bowl. Add the brown sugar mixture and mix well. Chill until serving time. Stir in the cilantro just before serving. May add pineapple if desired.

ITALIAN LASAGNA

1 pound Italian sausage

8 ounces ground beef

1 cup chopped onion

1 (28-ounce) can tomatoes, chopped

2 (6-ounce) cans tomato paste

$1^1/_2$ teaspoons basil

$^1/_8$ teaspoon garlic powder

15 ounces ricotta cheese

1 egg, beaten

1 tablespoon parsley flakes

1 large package lasagna noodles, cooked, drained

1 pound mozzarella cheese, shredded

$^3/_4$ cup grated Parmesan cheese

BROWN the sausage and ground beef with the onion in a large skillet, stirring until the sausage and ground beef are crumbly; drain. Stir in the next 4 ingredients. Bring to a boil; reduce the heat. Simmer for 20 minutes. Mix the ricotta cheese, egg and parsley flakes in a bowl. Spoon $1^1/_2$ cups of the meat sauce into a 9x13-inch baking dish. Layer the noodles, remaining meat sauce, ricotta mixture, mozzarella cheese and Parmesan cheese $^1/_3$ at a time in the baking dish. Bake, covered with foil, at 375 degrees for 25 minutes. Bake, uncovered, for 20 minutes. Let stand for 10 minutes before slicing. Yield: 6 servings.

MAIN DISHES

COLUMBUS BAR'S CODFISH FILLET SANDWICH

2 eggs

1 cup beer or ale

$^{1}/_{2}$ cup milk

$^{1}/_{2}$ cup baking mix

1 tablespoon Old Bay seasoning

1 tablespoon finely chopped dill

Salt and pepper to taste

1 cup vegetable oil

1 (6-ounce) codfish fillet

1 hamburger bun

1 lettuce leaf

1 tomato slice

Tartar sauce

WHISK the eggs in a bowl until fluffy. Add the beer, milk, baking mix, Old Bay seasoning, dill, salt and pepper and mix well. Let stand for 15 minutes. The batter should be the consistency of a thin pancake batter. Heat the oil in a deep skillet. Dip the fish into the batter; hold the fish over the batter to allow any excess to drip off. Place the fish gently in the skillet. Fry until golden brown, turning once; drain. Serve on the bun with lettuce, tomato and tartar sauce. Garnish with lemon wedges and a sprig of fresh dill. Yield: 1 serving.

FISKEFRIKADELLER (FISH BURGER)

1 cup chopped fish

$^1/_2$ cup flour

2 eggs

$^1/_4$ cup skim milk

1 teaspoon sea salt

1 teaspoon white pepper

1 teaspoon hot sauce

1 teaspoon very finely chopped dill

$^1/_4$ cup olive oil

GRIND the fish in a food processor until of the consistency of ground beef. Add the flour, eggs, skim milk, sea salt, pepper, hot sauce and dill. Process until the mixture resembles meat loaf. Shape into patties. Heat the oil in a nonstick skillet. Add the fish patties. Sauté for 3 to 4 minutes or until golden brown, turning twice. For a fish soufflé, increase the skim milk to $^1/_2$ cup; whip the egg whites separately and fold them into the fish mixture. Pour the mixture into a round mold sprayed with nonstick cooking spray. Place the mold over boiling water in a double boiler. Cook over low heat until a wooden pick inserted near the center comes out clean. Loosen the mixture from the mold with a knife. Invert gently onto a large plate. Garnish with lemon slices and marinated vegetables. May use any leftover or inexpensive fish in this recipe. Yield: 2 servings.

WHEN EERO SAARINEN DESIGNED THE IRWIN UNION BANK IN 1954, HE ALSO DESIGNED ITS FURNITURE. THE ORIGINAL DESKS COULD NOT ACCOMMODATE COMPUTERS, SO NEW DESKS WERE CREATED, ADHERING AS CLOSELY AS POSSIBLE TO THE ORIGINAL DESIGN.

MAIN DISHES

FETTUCCINI WITH FRESH GOAT CHEESE, RED PEPPER AND SCALLOPS

2 tablespoons butter

$^3/_4$ cup julienned red bell pepper

$^1/_2$ cup leeks, chopped

1 (4-ounce) log fresh goat cheese, crumbled

$^1/_2$ cup whipping cream

Salt, black pepper and cayenne to taste

4 servings uncooked fettuccini

1 pound scallops or shrimp, or mixed scallops and shrimp

2 tablespoons butter

MELT 2 tablespoons butter in a sauté pan. Add the red pepper and leeks. Sauté for 5 minutes or until tender. Stir in the cheese and whipping cream. Cook until heated through, stirring constantly. Season with salt, black pepper and cayenne. Cook the fettuccini in boiling water to cover in a saucepan; drain. Sauté the scallops in 2 tablespoons butter in a sauté pan until opaque. Add the fettuccini and red pepper sauce. Cook until heated through, stirring constantly. May replace part of the butter with olive oil. Yield: 4 servings.

BARBECUED SHRIMP

24 large shrimp, peeled, deveined, with tails intact

1 large onion, cut into 24 thin slices

24 slices bacon

2 tablespoons brown sugar

2 tablespoons soy sauce

2 tablespoons dry sherry

3 cloves of garlic, minced

$1/2$ teaspoon chili powder

$1/2$ teaspoon ground ginger

$1/2$ teaspoon salt

Shredded lettuce

CUT the shrimp along the inside curve and open out butterfly-style. Place 1 onion piece on 1 side of each shrimp. Wrap 1 bacon slice around each shrimp, securing with a wooden pick. Mix the brown sugar, soy sauce, sherry, garlic, chili powder, ginger and salt in a bowl. Dip the shrimp into the mixture. Let stand on a barbecue rack or broiling tray for 30 minutes. Grill over medium coals or broil for 5 minutes or until the shrimp turn pink and the bacon is crisp. Serve on a bed of shredded lettuce. Yield: 6 servings.

SHRIMP CREOLE

6 slices bacon

4 ribs celery, chopped

1 large onion, chopped

1 clove of garlic, chopped

1 (10-ounce) can tomato soup

1 soup can water

1 can tomato sauce

1 jar mushrooms

2 pounds shrimp, peeled, deveined, broken into pieces

$1/8$ teaspoon Tabasco sauce, or to taste

FRY the bacon in a skillet until crisp. Drain and crumble the bacon. Sauté the celery, onion and garlic in the bacon drippings in the skillet. Add the soup, water, tomato sauce, mushrooms and bacon and mix well. Simmer for 30 minutes. Add the shrimp and mix well. Simmer for 15 minutes. Season with Tabasco sauce. Serve over hot cooked rice.
Yield: 6 servings.

MAIN DISHES

FETA SHRIMP

This recipe came from architect Gunnar Birkerts.

 2 large onions, thinly sliced

 $^1/_3$ cup olive oil

 4 large tomatoes, peeled, coarsely chopped

 3 tablespoons finely chopped parsley

 $^1/_2$ teaspoon dried dillweed

 $^1/_4$ teaspoon sugar

 $^1/_8$ teaspoon freshly ground pepper

 1 clove of garlic, minced

 2 pounds large shrimp, peeled, deveined

 12 ounces feta cheese

 1 large tomato, peeled

 Chopped parsley or dillweed

SAUTE the onions in the oil in an ovenproof skillet. Add the chopped tomatoes, 3 tablespoons parsley, dillweed, sugar, pepper and garlic and mix well. Simmer, covered, for 30 minutes, stirring occasionally. Add the shrimp, dipping them into the sauce in the skillet and arranging in a circle. Crumble the cheese over the shrimp. Place the whole tomato in the center. Bake at 450 degrees for 10 to 15 minutes or until the shrimp turn pink and the cheese melts. Garnish with additional parsley. Yield: 6 to 8 servings.

GUNNAR BIRKERTS OF BIRMINGHAM, MICHIGAN, DESIGNED LINCOLN ELEMENTARY SCHOOL IN 1967. AN AERIAL VIEW OF LINCOLN SCHOOL WOULD SHOW A SQUARE WITHIN A CIRCLE WITHIN A SQUARE. THE PLAY AREA FOR THE YOUNGER CHILDREN IS WITHIN THE CIRCLE CLOSE TO THE SCHOOL, WHILE THE MAIN PLAYGROUND FOR THE OLDER CHILDREN IS OUTSIDE THE CIRCLE. IN 1988 BIRKERTS DESIGNED THE NEW ST. PETER'S LUTHERAN CHURCH, LOCATED ACROSS THE STREET FROM LINCOLN ELEMENTARY, WITH A 186-FOOT COPPER-CLAD SPIRE PROVIDING A MAGNIFICENT ADDITION TO THE SKYLINE OF DOWNTOWN COLUMBUS.

ALDIE'S SHRIMP CURRY

This recipe came from architects Mary Ann Thompson and Charles Rose.

2 medium Vidalia onions, chopped

2 medium Granny Smith apples, cubed

4 cloves of garlic, chopped

$^1/_2$ cup unsalted butter

1 tablespoon (heaping) chopped ginger

1 teaspoon chili powder

8 teaspoons flour

1 tablespoon (heaping) curry powder

4 cups chicken stock

1 pound large shrimp, peeled, deveined

$^1/_2$ avocado, chopped (optional)

Chopped fresh parsley (optional)

SAUTE the onions, apples and garlic in the butter in a skillet. Add the ginger and chili powder. Cook until the apples are tender. Add the flour and curry powder and mix well. Add the chicken stock gradually, stirring until smooth. Add the shrimp and mix well. Simmer until heated through. Sprinkle with the avocado and parsley just before serving. Serve with chutney, steamed rice and a green salad with vinaigrette dressing. May use raisins, peanuts and shredded coconut as optional condiments. Yield: 4 servings.

THE NEWEST ADDITION TO THIS CITY'S ROLL CALL OF OUTSTANDING CONTEMPORARY ARCHITECTURE IS THE BARTHOLOMEW COUNTY MEMORIAL FOR VETERANS. A LANDSCAPED SPACE OCCUPYING THREE-QUARTERS OF THE COURTHOUSE BLOCK, THE MEMORIAL'S CENTERPIECE IS A FORMATION OF 25 LIMESTONE COLUMNS, EACH 40 FEET TALL. INSCRIBED ON THE OUTER RING OF THE INNER COLUMNS ARE THE NAMES OF 171 INDIVIDUALS FROM BARTHOLOMEW COUNTY WHO DIED IN THE WARS OF THE TWENTIETH CENTURY. THE CENTER COLUMNS ARE DEDICATED TO EXCERPTS OF LETTERS WRITTEN TO, BY OR ABOUT THOSE WHO DIED IN SERVICE. ANOTHER KEY ELEMENT IN THE PROJECT IS A VETERANS WALK OF HONOR—A BLOCK-LONG BRICK PATH CONTAINING THE NAMES, RANKS, MILITARY BRANCHES AND DATES OF SERVICE OF MORE THAN 3,800 VETERANS. THE INSCRIBED BRICKS WERE PURCHASED BY OR FOR VETERANS WITH TIES TO BARTHOLOMEW COUNTY. THE MEMORIAL CONCEPT WAS A JOINT VENTURE OF DESIGN FIRMS THOMPSON AND ROSE OF CAMBRIDGE, MASSACHUSETTS, AND MICHAEL VAN VALKENBURGH AND ASSOCIATES, ALSO OF CAMBRIDGE. THEIR DESIGN WAS CHOSEN BECAUSE THE CONCEPT OF THE 25-COLUMN FORMATION IN WHICH THE NAMES AND MESSAGES OF WAR DEAD WERE SO PROMINENTLY DISPLAYED REPRESENTED THE ORIGINAL INTENTION—TO PROVIDE THE COMMUNITY WITH A PERSONAL MEMORY OF THE SACRIFICES MADE BY ALL VETERANS.

MAIN DISHES

LOUISIANA-STYLE SHRIMP

1 teaspoon chopped onion

2 tablespoons butter

$^2/_3$ cup shrimp pieces

$^2/_3$ cup hot cooked rice

$^2/_3$ cup whipping cream

$^1/_2$ teaspoon salt

$^1/_4$ teaspoon celery salt

Cayenne to taste

3 tablespoons catsup or chili sauce (optional)

COOK the onion in the butter in a skillet for 5 minutes, stirring constantly. Add the shrimp, rice and whipping cream and mix gently. Cook until heated through, stirring frequently. Add the salt, celery salt, cayenne and catsup and mix well. Cook until heated through. Seasonings may be varied to taste.

Yield: 4 to 6 servings.

LILLIAN C. SCHMITT ELEMENTARY SCHOOL, BUILT IN 1957, WAS THE FIRST SCHOOL CONSTRUCTED UNDER THE CUMMINS ENGINE FOUNDATION ARCHITECTURAL PROGRAM. IT WAS ALSO THE FIRST SCHOOL IN A SERIES OF NEW SCHOOLS NAMED IN HONOR OF LOCAL EDUCATORS. MISS LILLIAN SCHMITT (1891-1959) WAS AN ELEMENTARY TEACHER IN THE LOCAL SCHOOLS FOR 43 YEARS.

SHRIMP IN SOUR CREAM

2 cups cooked shrimp

2 (4-ounce) cans sliced mushrooms, drained, or sliced fresh mushrooms

$1/4$ cup butter

1 cup sour cream

$1^1/2$ teaspoons salt

1 teaspoon Worcestershire sauce

1 teaspoon dried dillweed, or 1 tablespoon fresh

1 teaspoon paprika

1 tablespoon flour

6 to 8 servings hot cooked rice

$1/4$ cup fresh lemon juice

HEAT the shrimp and mushrooms in the butter in a skillet, stirring gently occasionally. Mix the sour cream, salt, Worcestershire sauce, dillweed, paprika and flour in a bowl. Pour over the shrimp mixture. Cook until heated through. Serve over the rice. Sprinkle with the lemon juice. Garnish with lemon slices and fresh dill. Yield: 6 to 8 servings.

FETTUCCINI ALFREDO

8 ounces cream cheese, cubed, softened

$3/4$ cup grated Parmesan cheese

$1/2$ cup butter, softened

$1/2$ cup milk

8 ounces fettuccini, cooked, drained

Chopped cooked ham or bacon (optional)

COMBINE the cream cheese, Parmesan cheese, butter and milk in a saucepan. Cook over low heat until thickened, stirring constantly until smooth. Toss with the fettuccini in a bowl. Stir in the ham.
Yield: 4 to 5 servings.

MAIN DISHES

LASAGNA CALZONES

Vegetable oil

8 ounces mushrooms, sliced

$^1/_2$ cup chopped onion

1 (16-ounce) can Grands! buttermilk biscuits

8 ounces ricotta cheese

$^1/_2$ cup shredded mozzarella cheese

1 (32-ounce) jar spaghetti sauce

$^1/_2$ cup grated Parmesan cheese

HEAT a small amount of oil in a skillet. Add the mushrooms and onion. Stir-fry for 7 minutes or until tender. Work with 1 biscuit at a time. Flatten the biscuit on a baking sheet and stretch into a 6- to 7-inch circle. Layer 2 tablespoons ricotta cheese, 2 tablespoons mushroom mixture, 1 tablespoon mozzarella cheese, 2 tablespoons spaghetti sauce and 2 teaspoons Parmesan cheese on 1 half of the biscuit. Fold the other half over the filling, using a fork to hold in the filling. Pinch the edges together to seal. Repeat with the remaining biscuits. Bake at 375 degrees for 15 to 20 minutes or until golden brown. Drizzle with the remaining spaghetti sauce. Sprinkle with the remaining Parmesan cheese.

Yield: 8 servings.

THE "RIVER RATS" ARE COLUMBUS VOLUNTEERS WHO, IN 1960, JOINED WITH OTHERS TO CLEAN UP "DEATH VALLEY," THE SWAMPY LAND BY THE RIVER. THE "RATS" DID THE HARD WORK OF PULLING LOGS FROM THE WATER AND HAULING DEBRIS, HELPING TO CREATE WHAT IS NOW MILL RACE PARK. TODAY, THE "RIVER RATS" CONTINUE THEIR CLEANUP WORK AS WELL AS RAISE FUNDS TO AID COMMUNITY PROJECTS.

PENNE WITH VODKA AND SPICY TOMATO CREAM SAUCE

$1/4$ cup virgin olive oil

2 Italian sausages

4 cloves of garlic, minced

$1/2$ teaspoon crushed red pepper

1 (28-ounce) can crushed tomatoes

$3/4$ teaspoon salt

1 pound penne

Salt to taste

2 teaspoons vodka

$1/2$ cup whipping cream

$1/4$ cup chopped fresh parsley

HEAT the oil in a large skillet. Add the sausage. Cook until brown, stirring until crumbly; drain. Add the garlic and red pepper. Cook until the garlic is golden brown. Add the tomatoes and $3/4$ teaspoon salt. Bring to a boil; reduce the heat. Simmer for 15 minutes. Cook the pasta in boiling salted water in a stockpot until al dente; drain. Return the pasta to the stockpot. Add the vodka and whipping cream to the sauce in the skillet. Bring to a boil. Stir into the pasta. Cook over low heat for 1 minute. Stir in the parsley. Yield: 4 servings.

INTEREST IN—AND COMMITMENT TO—QUALITY LED TO THE 1964 STOREFRONT RENOVATION PROGRAM IN DOWNTOWN COLUMBUS. ALEXANDER GIRARD, AN ARCHITECT KNOWN FOR HIS OUTSTANDING USE OF COLOR, DESIGNED THIS PROGRAM WHEREBY MERCHANTS HAVE RENOVATED AND RESTORED THEIR NINETEENTH-CENTURY MIDWESTERN BUILDINGS. RENOVATION CONTINUES TODAY TO CONVERT UPPER FLOURS TO HOUSING.

MAIN DISHES

BROCCOLI WITH ZITI

8 ounces ziti

1 bunch broccoli, cut into 1-inch pieces

1 cup (or more) any type chopped ham

2 fresh tomatoes, chopped, or equivalent amount of cherry tomato halves

$1/2$ cup (or more) freshly grated Parmesan cheese

3 cloves of garlic, chopped

1 teaspoon red pepper flakes

$1/4$ cup olive oil

1 tablespoon margarine

Salt, garlic salt and black pepper to taste

COOK the pasta in boiling water in a large saucepan using the package directions; drain. Steam or quickly cook the broccoli until tender-crisp; drain. Toss the pasta, broccoli, ham, tomatoes and cheese in a clear glass bowl. Heat the garlic, red pepper flakes, oil and margarine in a small saucepan or skillet. Pour over the pasta mixture and toss gently to coat. Season with salt, garlic salt and black pepper. Serve immediately with additional red pepper flakes and freshly ground Parmesan cheese on the side. Recipe may be doubled or tripled. Yield: 4 to 6 servings.

SUMMERTIME PASTA

This recipe came from architect Robert Venturi, who says, "Here is a vague kind of recipe for a simple kind of pasta containing elemental summer ingredients that I occasionally prepare for supper on Sundays deriving from vague memories growing up in a quasi-Italo-American household and from vivid memories of meals in trattorias when a student in Rome."

Any kind of pasta, cooked al dente

Crushed and drained ripe tomatoes

Crushed fresh basil

Good quality strong-flavored olive oil

A very very subtle amount of crushed fresh garlic

Salt

THE last ingredients should be proportioned discreetly and applied cold to the first ingredient, which is hot.

J.R.'S BARBECUE SAUCE

4 large white onions, chopped

$1/2$ gallon catsup

$1/4$ cup hot sauce

3 tablespoons white vinegar

$2 1/2$ cups packed brown sugar

$1/4$ cup lemon juice

1 cup sugar

$1/2$ gallon Open Pit barbecue sauce (original flavor)

$1/4$ cup Worcestershire sauce

COMBINE the onions, catsup, hot sauce, vinegar, brown sugar, lemon juice, sugar, barbecue sauce and Worcestershire sauce in an 8-quart saucepan. Bring to a boil; reduce the heat. Simmer for 30 to 45 minutes or until heated through. Let cool. Cover and store in the refrigerator for 2 weeks before using.
Yield: 5 to 6 quarts.

IN 1967 ROBERT VENTURI OF VENTURI & RAUCH, PHILADELPHIA, PENNSYLVANIA, DESIGNED FIRE STATION NO. 4, WITH A HOSE DRYING TOWER THAT PROVIDES A FOCAL POINT AGAINST AN OTHERWISE LOW BUILDING.

MAIN DISHES

CHEF JAMES GREGORY'S ROMESCO SAUCE

1 cup almonds, lightly toasted

2 red bell peppers, roasted, peeled, seeded

1 teaspoon salt

2 teaspoons ground cumin

2 teaspoons red wine vinegar

1 cup olive oil

PROCESS the almonds in a food processor until fine crumbs form. Add the bell peppers. Process until puréed. Add the salt, cumin and vinegar. Pulse until blended. Drizzle in the oil with the food processor running, processing until smooth. Keeps well in the refrigerator for several days. Serve over chicken, fish or vegetables. Yie!d: 6 to 8 servings.

HERB STEAK BUTTER

$^1/_2$ cup butter or margarine, softened

1 teaspoon chopped chives

1 teaspoon dillweed

1 teaspoon paprika

$^1/_2$ teaspoon salt

$^1/_2$ teaspoon garlic powder

$^1/_4$ teaspoon pepper

1 teaspoon fresh lemon juice

MIX the butter, chives, dillweed, paprika, salt, garlic powder and pepper in a bowl. Stir in the lemon juice. Spread on steaks just after grilling or use as a sauce for beef fondue. Yield: $^3/_4$ cup.

SIDE DISHES

SIDE DISHES

CONTENTS

LOCATED IN THE COMMONS IS
THE KINETIC SCULPTURE "CHAOS I,"
1974, BY JEAN TINQUELY.

ARTICHOKE WIGGLE

1/2 block (about) extra-sharp
Cheddar cheese

2 (10-ounce) cans artichoke hearts,
drained

2 tablespoons (heaping) mayonnaise

2 or 3 eggs, beaten

Salt and pepper to taste

1/2 package (about) extra-wide egg
noodles, cooked, drained, rinsed

1 tomato, thinly sliced

1/2 cup Italian bread crumbs

SHRED the cheese in a food processor. Add the artichoke hearts. Process until coarsely sliced but not ground. Pour into a large bowl. Add the mayonnaise and eggs and mix well. Season with salt and pepper. Add the noodles and mix gently. Spoon into a 9x12-inch glass casserole sprayed with nonstick cooking spray. Top with the tomato slices. Sprinkle with the bread crumbs. Bake at 350 degrees for 30 minutes or until the mixture is heated through and the noodles are tender. Broil briefly until the top is brown. Ingredient amounts in this recipe may be increased or decreased depending on your taste.
Yield: 6 servings.

ARTICHOKE SPINACH CASSEROLE

1 (15-ounce) can artichoke hearts,
drained, cut into halves

1 tablespoon butter

3 (10-ounce) packages frozen chopped
spinach

8 ounces cream cheese, softened

1 teaspoon salt

1/2 teaspoon pepper

1 cup chopped onion

1 cup shredded Swiss cheese

Paprika to taste

SAUTE the artichoke hearts in the butter in a skillet. Let cool. Cook the spinach using the package directions; drain well. Mix the spinach, artichoke hearts, cream cheese, salt, pepper and onion in a bowl. Spoon into a 2-quart baking dish. Top with the Swiss cheese. Sprinkle with paprika. Bake at 350 degrees for 30 minutes. Yield: 6 to 8 servings.

SIDE DISHES

HOLLY'S BAKED BEANS

2 (30-ounce) cans baked beans

1 pound bacon, crisp-cooked, crumbled

1 1/2 cups packed brown sugar

1/2 cup catsup

2 teaspoons dry mustard

MIX the beans, bacon, brown sugar, catsup and mustard in a bowl. Spoon into a large casserole. Bake at 200 degrees for 5 hours or at 325 degrees for 2 1/2 hours. May instead be prepared in a slow cooker.
Yield: 8 to 10 servings.

SWEET-AND-SOUR BAKED BEANS

2 cans butter beans, drained

1 can baked beans, drained

1 can green lima beans, drained

1 can red kidney beans, drained

1 onion, sliced into rings

1 teaspoon dry mustard

1 1/2 cups packed brown sugar

1 teaspoon garlic powder

1/2 cup vinegar

1 teaspoon salt

8 slices bacon, crisp-cooked, crumbled

COMBINE all the beans in a bowl and mix well. Spoon into a 9x13-inch casserole. Combine the onion, mustard, brown sugar, garlic powder, vinegar and salt in a saucepan. Simmer for 20 minutes. Pour over the beans. Top with the bacon. Bake at 350 degrees for 1 hour. Good served with honey-baked ham.
Yield: 8 to 10 servings.

THE HAMILTON CENTER, AN ICE SKATING AND RECREATIONAL CENTER BUILT IN 1958, IS A GIFT TO THE COMMUNITY FROM THE HAMILTON FOUNDATION AS A MEMORIAL TO B. F. HAMILTON, FOUNDER OF COSCO, INC. THE FOUNDATION CONTRIBUTED THIS TYPE OF CENTER BECAUSE THE COMMUNITY LACKED RECREATIONAL FACILITIES FOR THE WINTER MONTHS. THE ICE SKATING RINK WAS ENCLOSED IN 1975 SO THE COMMUNITY COULD ENJOY THIS FACILITY YEAR ROUND.

CAJUN SKILLET BEANS

1 medium onion, chopped

3 cloves of garlic, minced

2 tablespoons vegetable oil

3 ribs celery, chopped

2 green or red bell peppers, chopped

1 teaspoon chopped fresh thyme, or
1^1/$_2$ teaspoons dried

1 tablespoon chopped fresh basil, or
1 teaspoon dried

1 teaspoon chopped fresh oregano, or
^{1}/$_2$ teaspoon dried

^{1}/$_4$ teaspoon pepper, or to taste

^{1}/$_8$ teaspoon cayenne, or to taste

^{1}/$_8$ teaspoon salt, or to taste

2 cups chopped fresh or canned tomatoes

1 tablespoon honey or molasses

1 tablespoon Dijon mustard

4 cups cooked canned or frozen black-
eyed peas or butter beans

Chopped scallions

Grated cheese

SAUTE the onion and garlic in the oil in a
heavy skillet over medium heat. Add the
celery and green peppers. Cook for 5 minutes,
stirring occasionally. Add the thyme, basil,
oregano, pepper, cayenne and salt. Cook,
covered, for 5 minutes or until the onion is
golden brown, stirring once or twice. Add the
tomatoes, honey and Dijon mustard. Simmer
for 5 minutes. Add the peas. Cook, covered,
until heated through, stirring occasionally.
Sprinkle with scallions and cheese.
Yield: 6 servings.

NANCY'S GREEN BEANS

1 pound fresh green beans, trimmed,
broken into pieces

1 pound bacon, cut into 1-inch pieces

1 medium onion, chopped

1 (8-ounce) can sliced mushrooms

1 (8-ounce) can sliced water chestnuts,
drained, chopped (optional)

COOK the beans in water to cover in a
saucepan until tender; drain. Cook the bacon
in a large skillet until crisp; drain, reserving
2 tablespoons drippings. Cook the onion in
the reserved drippings in the skillet until
tender. Add the mushrooms, water chestnuts
and bacon. Add the green beans and mix well.
Cook until heated through. May substitute
frozen green beans for fresh.
Yield: 4 to 6 servings.

SIDE DISHES

BARB'S BROCCOLI AND RICE

1 (6-ounce) package long grain and wild rice

1 (16-ounce) package frozen broccoli, thawed, drained

1 (10-ounce) can cream of chicken soup

1 (8-ounce) can sliced water chestnuts, drained

$^1/_2$ cup milk

1 (8-ounce) jar Cheez Whiz

COOK the rice using the package directions. Combine with the broccoli, soup, water chestnuts, milk and half the Cheez Whiz in a bowl and mix well. Spoon into a 2-quart casserole. Spread with the remaining Cheez Whiz. Bake at 350 degrees for 40 minutes.
Yield: 4 to 6 servings.

CARROTS AU GRATIN

3 cups cooked sliced carrots

1 (10-ounce) can cream of celery soup

1 cup shredded Cheddar cheese

$^1/_4$ cup dry bread crumbs

1 tablespoon melted butter

MIX the carrots, soup and cheese in a bowl. Spoon into a buttered 2-quart casserole. Sprinkle with a mixture of the bread crumbs and melted butter. Bake at 350 degrees for 25 minutes. Yield: 6 servings.

126

CARROTS WITH CRANBERRIES AND MINT

1 pound carrots, julienned, or 1 pound baby carrots

1 cup water

$1/8$ teaspoon salt, or to taste

1 tablespoon sugar

$1/4$ cup dried cranberries

2 teaspoons vegetable oil

$1/2$ teaspoon dried mint

COMBINE the carrots, water and salt in a saucepan. Cover and bring to a boil. Simmer just until tender. Add the sugar, cranberries and oil. Simmer until the liquid is absorbed and the cranberries are plump. Stir in the mint. Yield: 4 to 5 servings.

CORN APLENTY

1 (9-ounce) package corn muffin mix

1 can cream-style corn

1 can whole kernel corn, drained

1 egg

1 cup sour cream

$1/2$ cup melted margarine

COMBINE the corn muffin mix, corn, egg, sour cream and margarine in a bowl and mix well. Spoon into a 2-quart casserole. Bake at 350 degrees for 50 minutes or until light brown. Yield: 8 servings.

A HIGHLIGHT OF THE COMMONS IS THE "IN MOTION" SCULPTURE "CHAOS I," CREATED BY JEAN TINGUELY IN 1974. IN RECOMMENDING A MAJOR WORK OF ART FOR THE COMMONS, ARCHITECT CESAR PELLI STATED, "WE WOULD LIKE A GREAT MAGNET, A FOCAL POINT SUCH AS THE OLD TOWN CLOCK . . . A PLACE FOR PEOPLE TO MEET AND GREET ONE ANOTHER."

SIDE DISHES

SCALLOPED CORN AND SAUSAGE

$^1/_2$ cup sausage

1 cup crushed crackers

1 (20-ounce) can cream-style corn

$^1/_2$ cup milk

Salt and pepper to taste

BROWN the sausage in a skillet, stirring until crumbly; drain, reserving the drippings. Mix the reserved drippings with the cracker crumbs in a bowl. Mix the corn and milk in a bowl. Sprinkle $^1/_3$ of the crumbs in a greased 8x8-inch casserole. Spread half the corn mixture over the crumbs. Season with salt and pepper. Add layers of half the sausage, half the remaining crumbs, remaining corn mixture, remaining sausage and remaining crumbs. Bake at 350 degrees for 30 minutes. Yield: 6 servings.

CHEESY CORN CASSEROLE

2 cups fresh or frozen corn

$^1/_2$ cup melted butter

2 eggs

1 cup sour cream

1 cup chopped Monterey Jack or mozzarella cheese

$^1/_2$ cup cornmeal

1$^1/_2$ teaspoons salt

MIX the corn, butter, eggs, sour cream, cheese, cornmeal and salt in a bowl. Spoon into a buttered 7x11-inch baking dish. Bake at 350 degrees for 45 minutes or until puffed and beginning to brown. Yield: 6 to 8 servings.

FROZEN FRESH SWEET CORN

6 to 8 ears of fresh sweet corn

2 teaspoons salt

8 quarts water

1 tablespoon (or more) butter

Salt and pepper to taste

2 teaspoons (or more) sugar, or equivalent amount of artificial sweetener

REMOVE the husks and silks from the corn. Bring the salted water to a rapid boil in a 12-quart kettle. Add the corn. Blanch for 10 minutes. Remove the corn and plunge immediately into cold water. Let stand until the corn is cool enough to handle. Cut the kernels from the ears with a sharp knife. Place the corn in freezer bags, leaving $1/2$ inch headspace; seal. Use pint bags for families of 4, quart bags for larger families. Freeze until needed. To serve, place the corn in the microwave in the bag. Defrost for 1 minute. Place the corn in a microwave-safe dish. Microwave on High for 5 minutes. Add the butter, salt to taste, pepper and sugar. Microwave on High for 2 to 3 minutes or until the butter melts and the corn is hot.
Yield: 4 to 6 servings.

BAKED MUSHROOMS

24 large mushrooms

1 onion, finely chopped

$1/4$ cup butter

Salt and pepper to taste

2 slices dry bread, crumbled

$3/4$ cup whipping cream

WIPE the mushrooms with a damp cloth. Remove and chop the stems. Place the mushroom caps in a shallow 8x12-inch baking dish. Sauté the onion and mushroom stems in the butter in a skillet. Season with salt and pepper. Add the bread crumbs and mix well. Spoon into the mushroom caps. Pour the whipping cream around the mushroom caps. Bake at 350 degrees for 45 minutes or until the whipping cream is thickened and brown.
Yield: 6 servings.

SIDE DISHES

MARINATED MUSHROOMS WITH LITTLE GREEN SAUCE

1 cup chopped parsley

2 cloves of garlic, finely chopped

1 teaspoon salt

$1/2$ teaspoon pepper

2 teaspoons Dijon mustard

$1/2$ teaspoon celery seeds

$1^1/2$ cups very fruity extra-virgin olive oil

Red wine vinegar

Sliced fresh white mushrooms

COMBINE the parsley, garlic, salt, pepper, Dijon mustard, celery seeds and oil in a bowl or tightly covered jar and mix vigorously. Add the vinegar and mix well. Adjust the salt and vinegar. The sauce should be rather thick and taste slightly salty and vinegary. Pour over the mushrooms in a bowl and mix well to coat. Marinate, covered, in the refrigerator for 2 hours or longer, mixing several times. Mix again just before serving. The sauce may also be used to accompany boiled beef, chicken, hot boiled potatoes or sliced tomatoes.

Yield: 4 to 6 servings.

HENRY MOORE'S SCULPTURE "LARGE ARCH" IS THE CENTERPIECE OF THE CLEO ROGERS MEMORIAL LIBRARY PLAZA. MR. MOORE, CONSIDERED ONE OF THE GREATEST ARTISTS OF THE TWENTIETH CENTURY, WAS 73 YEARS OLD WHEN HE CREATED "LARGE ARCH." HE SAID, "AS A YOUNG SCULPTOR I SAW STONEHENGE AND EVER SINCE I'VE WANTED TO DO WORK THAT COULD BE WALKED THROUGH AND AROUND."

ROASTED POTATOES

This recipe came from exhibit designer Tony Spagnola.

6 tablespoons olive oil

6 cloves of garlic, minced

1 teaspoon salt

$1/2$ teaspoon pepper

$1/2$ teaspoon dried thyme

$1/4$ teaspoon dried rosemary

$2 1/2$ pounds medium red potatoes, cut into quarters

5 tablespoons olive oil

2 tablespoons white vinegar

2 teaspoons Dijon mustard

$1/4$ cup chopped shallots

COMBINE 6 tablespoons oil, garlic, salt, pepper, thyme and rosemary in a large bowl and mix well. Add the potatoes and toss to coat. Spoon into a baking dish. Bake at 375 degrees for 55 minutes or until brown. Remove the potatoes to a bowl and let cool. Mix 5 tablespoons oil and 1 tablespoon of the pan drippings in a small bowl. Whisk in the vinegar and Dijon mustard. Add the shallots and mix well. Pour over the potatoes. May be prepared up to 6 hours ahead; let stand at room temperature for 1 hour before serving. Yield: 6 servings.

TONY SPAGNOLA OF SPAGNOLA AND ASSOCIATES, NEW YORK CITY, DESIGNED ONE OF THE MANY NEW FEATURES IN THE NEWLY RENOVATED VISITORS CENTER. THE 1,250-SQUARE-FOOT EXHIBIT IS ENTITLED "COLUMBUS, INDIANA: PEOPLE AND THEIR BUILDINGS." IT FEATURES EIGHT PANELS OF TEXT AND PHOTOGRAPHS, TWO INTERACTIVE KIOSKS, AND SEVERAL BUILDING MODELS. SPAGNOLA SAYS THAT "THE EXHIBIT INCLUDES HISTORICAL SECTIONS SHOWING THE BEGINNING OF COLUMBUS AND NUMEROUS EXAMPLES OF THE NINETEENTH CENTURY ARCHITECTURE AS WELL AS MANY CONTEMPORARY BUILDINGS LOCATED IN COLUMBUS." PANELS REFLECT ON THE "PEOPLE AND THEIR BUILDINGS" THEME BY EXPLORING DIFFERENT TOPICS, INCLUDING THE HISTORY OF COLUMBUS, THE ART OF ARCHITECTURE, ARCHITECTS' WORK IN AND OUT OF COLUMBUS, CULTIVATION OF THE ARTS AND THE PROCESS OF ARCHITECTURE. SOME OF SPAGNOLA'S OTHER EXHIBITS ARE ON DISPLAY AT THE CUMMINS ENGINE COMPANY CORPORATE OFFICE BUILDING.

SIDE DISHES

FOIL POTATOES

4 large baking potatoes

$^1/_4$ cup butter

Seasoned salt and garlic salt to taste

Lemon pepper to taste

$^1/_4$ cup grated Parmesan cheese

CUT the potatoes into French fry-style strips. Spray the center of 4 large pieces of foil with nonstick cooking spray. Divide the potatoes among the foil squares. Top each with 1 tablespoon butter. Season with seasoned salt, garlic salt and lemon pepper. Sprinkle with the cheese. Fold the edges of the foil together tightly to seal. Place on a baking sheet. Bake at 350 degrees for 1 hour. Yield: 4 servings.

LOW-CALORIE POTATOES

3 potatoes, chopped

$1^1/_2$ cups chicken broth

2 cloves of garlic, minced

1 teaspoon basil

1 teaspoon seasoned salt

$^1/_4$ cup skim milk

$^1/_4$ cup chopped onion (optional)

BOIL the potatoes in the chicken broth in a saucepan; drain and rinse. Combine with the garlic, basil, seasoned salt, skim milk and onion in a bowl. Mash until of desired consistency. Yield: 4 servings.

FOR OVER 18 YEARS COLUMBUS RESIDENTS HAVE GATHERED TOGETHER TO ENJOY POPFEST, AN OUTDOOR MUSIC FESTIVAL. TWO ORCHESTRAS, FOOD AND DRINK, SINGERS, FAMILIES AND A WARM SUMMER DAY ARE THE PRIME INGREDIENTS OF POPFEST. CROWDS GATHER ON THE LIBRARY PLAZA AS SYMPHONY MUSIC FILLS THE DOWNTOWN AIR.

HOOSIER-STYLE TWICE-BAKED POTATOES

4 large Idaho baking potatoes

Shortening

2 green onions, chopped

4 ounces mild Colby cheese, shredded

$^1/_4$ cup butter or margarine

$^1/_4$ cup sour cream

2 tablespoons bacon bits

SCRUB the potatoes; rub with shortening. Wrap the potatoes in foil and pierce with a fork several times. Place on the center oven rack. Bake at 450 degrees for $1^1/_2$ hours. Remove from the oven and let cool. Reduce the oven temperature to 350 degrees. Cut a shallow lengthwise slit in the top of each potato. Scoop out the pulp, leaving the potato shells intact. Combine the potato pulp, green onions, cheese, butter, sour cream and bacon bits in a bowl and mash well. Spoon into the potato shells. Bake for 20 minutes.

Yield: 4 servings.

SUMMER SQUASH SURPRISE

4 or 5 green onions

3 to 4 tablespoons butter

2 pounds yellow summer squash, sliced

1 cup sour cream

SLICE the white bulb of the green onions; slice the green tops thinly and reserve for garnishing. Sauté the green onion bulbs in the butter in a saucepan. Add the squash. Cook over low heat just until tender. Spoon into a bowl. Fold in the sour cream just before serving. Beat until the sour cream is barely warm. Garnish with the reserved sliced green onion tops. Serve with grilled chicken.

Yield: 4 servings.

SIDE DISHES

SWEET POTATOES MAUI

3 tablespoons melted butter

2 cups mashed sweet potatoes

1 teaspoon grated orange peel

6 tablespoons orange juice

1 cup crushed pineapple

Salt to taste

Sliced bananas (optional)

2 tablespoons brown sugar

Paprika to taste

Flaked coconut (optional)

Brown sugar (optional)

WHIP the butter into the sweet potatoes in a bowl. Add the orange peel, orange juice, pineapple and salt and mix well. Place a layer of banana slices in a buttered 1-quart casserole. Spoon the sweet potato mixture over the bananas. Sprinkle with 2 tablespoons brown sugar and paprika. Bake, covered, at 350 degrees for 30 minutes. Sprinkle with coconut and additional brown sugar. Broil until brown. Yield: 6 servings.

GLAZED SWEET POTATOES

4 large sweet potatoes

Butter or margarine

2 cups sugar

2 tablespoons cornstarch

$1/8$ teaspoon salt, or to taste

$1/2$ cup light corn syrup

1 tablespoon vinegar

1 cup water

1 teaspoon vanilla extract

COOK the sweet potatoes in water to cover in a saucepan until tender. Peel the sweet potatoes and cut into slices. Place in a casserole. Dot with butter. Mix the sugar, cornstarch and salt in a saucepan. Add the corn syrup, vinegar and 1 cup water. Cook for 5 minutes, stirring occasionally. Stir in the vanilla. Pour over the sweet potatoes. Bake at 400 degrees for 30 minutes. Yield: 6 to 8 servings.

MRS. O'S GARLIC TOMATOES

3 to 4 tomatoes

4 cloves of garlic, cut into 2 to 3 slices each

Salt and pepper to taste

CUT the top and bottom off the tomatoes. Cut the tomatoes into quarters. Combine with the garlic, salt and pepper in a plastic container. Chill, covered, for 2 to 3 hours, stirring every 30 minutes. The garlic flavor intensifies the longer the mixture is refrigerated.

Yield: 3 to 4 servings.

TOMATO PIE

Sliced tomatoes

Sliced green onions

1 baked pie shell

Fresh or dried basil to taste

Salt and pepper to taste

1 cup mayonnaise

1 cup shredded sharp or mild Cheddar cheese

ALTERNATE layers of tomatoes and green onions in the pie shell until filled, sprinkling with basil, salt and pepper between each layer. Spread a mixture of the mayonnaise and cheese over the top, sealing to the edge. Bake at 350 degrees for 30 minutes or until the top is light brown. May use onions other than green onions, increasing the baking time until the onions are cooked through.

Yield: 6 to 8 servings.

"IT IS SAID THAT ARCHITECTURE IS FROZEN MUSIC, BUT SELDOM IN HISTORY HAS ANY GROUP OF DEVOTED ARTISTS PRODUCED SUCH A SYMPHONY IN STONE AS PRESENTS ITSELF TO THE EYE IN COLUMBUS."

—LADY BIRD JOHNSON

SIDE DISHES

STUFFED TOMATOES

4 medium tomatoes, cored, drained

3 slices bacon

$1/4$ cup chopped onion

8 ounces fresh spinach, snipped

$1/2$ cup sour cream

$1/8$ teaspoon hot pepper sauce, or to taste

Salt to taste

$1/2$ cup shredded mozzarella cheese

CUT the tops off the tomatoes. Remove the seeds and pulp from the center, reserving the shells; drain. Cook the bacon in a skillet until crisp; drain, reserving 2 tablespoons drippings. Crumble the bacon and set aside. Cook the onion in the reserved drippings in the skillet. Stir in the spinach. Cook, covered, for 3 to 5 minutes or until tender. Remove from the heat. Stir in the sour cream, hot pepper sauce and bacon. Sprinkle the tomatoes with salt. Fill with the spinach mixture. Place in an 8x8-inch baking dish. Bake at 375 degrees for 20 to 25 minutes or until heated through. Top with the cheese. Bake until the cheese melts. Yield: 4 servings.

BARLEY BAKE

2 tablespoons butter

1 cup barley

1 (4-ounce) can mushrooms

2 (10-ounce) cans onion soup

$1/2$ cup shredded Cheddar cheese

MELT the butter in a skillet. Add the barley. Cook until brown, stirring constantly. Add the undrained mushrooms and soup. Bring to a boil. Spoon into a 2-quart casserole. Bake, covered, at 350 degrees for 1 hour. Top with the cheese. Bake, uncovered, for 10 minutes or until the cheese melts. Yield: 8 servings.

MINUTE RICE

1$^1/_2$ cups instant rice

$^1/_4$ cup butter

$^3/_4$ cup water

$^1/_2$ cup chopped onion

1$^1/_2$ cans beef consommé

$^1/_4$ teaspoon MSG

$^1/_4$ teaspoon pepper

1 (8-ounce) can water chestnuts, drained

COMBINE the rice, butter, water, onion, consommé, MSG, pepper and water chestnuts in a saucepan and mix well. Cook, covered, for 15 minutes. Yield: 4 servings.

PINE NUT AND GREEN ONION RICE PILAF

2 cups rice

1 cup sliced green onions

1 cup pine nuts

$^1/_4$ cup margarine or butter

5 cups chicken broth

2 teaspoons grated lemon peel

$^1/_2$ teaspoon salt

$^1/_2$ cup sliced green onion tops

COOK the rice, green onions and pine nuts in the margarine in a 3-quart saucepan for 5 minutes or until the pine nuts are light brown, stirring frequently. Stir in the chicken broth, lemon peel and salt. Bring to a boil, stirring once or twice; reduce the heat. Simmer, covered, for 14 minutes; do not lift the cover or stir. Remove from the heat. Fluff the rice lightly with a fork. Let stand, covered, for 5 to 10 minutes or until steamed. Spoon into a bowl. Sprinkle with the green onion tops. Yield: 12 servings.

SIDE DISHES

ROBIN WILLEY'S CHILI RICE

3 cups cooked long grain rice

Salt and freshly ground pepper to taste

3 cups sour cream

1 (4-ounce) can chopped green chiles

$^1/_2$ to 1 can sliced jalapeños, chopped

12 ounces Monterey Jack cheese, sliced

$^1/_2$ cup shredded Cheddar cheese

SEASON the rice with salt and pepper. Combine the sour cream, green chiles, jalapeños and salt in a bowl and mix well. Layer the rice, sour cream mixture and Monterey Jack cheese $^1/_3$ to $^1/_2$ at a time in a buttered $1^1/_2$-quart casserole, ending with the rice. Bake at 350 degrees for 40 to 45 minutes or until heated through. Sprinkle with the Cheddar cheese. Bake until the Cheddar cheese melts. May use low-fat or fat-free sour cream. Yield: 6 servings.

APPLESAUCE

5 pounds cooking apples

1 cup packed light brown sugar

1 cup apple cider

2 tablespoons lemon juice

$^1/_2$ teaspoon nutmeg

PEEL the apples and core. Cut each apple into 8 wedges. Place the apples in a large baking dish. Heat the brown sugar with the cider in a saucepan, stirring until the brown sugar dissolves. Remove from the heat. Stir in the lemon juice and nutmeg. Pour over the apples. Bake, covered, at 350 degrees for 45 minutes or until the apples are tender. Break the apples into the desired consistency with a fork. Yield: 6 to 8 servings.

JOYCE'S FRUIT FESTIVAL

1 (20-ounce) can pineapple tidbits

1 (11-ounce) can mandarin oranges, drained

3 medium apples, chopped

3 bananas, sliced

$^1/_2$ cup sugar

2 tablespoons cornstarch

$^1/_3$ cup orange juice

1 tablespoon lemon juice

1 tablespoon grated orange peel

DRAIN the pineapple, reserving $^3/_4$ cup juice. Combine the pineapple, oranges, apples and bananas in a large bowl. Mix the sugar and cornstarch in a saucepan. Add the reserved pineapple juice, orange juice, lemon juice and orange peel. Cook over medium heat until the mixture boils and thickens. Pour over the fruit while hot. Chill, uncovered, for several hours to overnight. Recipe may be doubled. May use any combination of fresh or canned fruit in season. Yield: 8 servings.

VINTON FARM MACARONI AND CHEESE

2 cups ziti, penne or other large macaroni

Salt to taste

2 tablespoons butter

2 tablespoons flour

1 teaspoon salt

$^1/_4$ teaspoon paprika

1 teaspoon dry mustard, or to taste

Red pepper flakes to taste

$1^1/_2$ cups whipping cream

8 ounces sharp Cheddar cheese, shredded

Shredded wheat

Melted butter

COOK the macaroni in boiling salted water in a saucepan for 20 minutes. Melt 2 table-spoons butter in a saucepan. Add the flour. Cook for 2 minutes, stirring constantly. Add 1 teaspoon salt, paprika, mustard, pepper and whipping cream. Cook until thickened, stirring occasionally. Add the cheese. Pour into a tall round ovenproof bowl. Add the macaroni and mix well. Mix the shredded wheat and melted butter in a bowl. Cover the macaroni mixture with the shredded wheat. Bake at 350 degrees for 30 minutes or until light brown. Recipe may be doubled. Yield: 4 servings.

SIDE DISHES

DARVEL'S OLD-FASHIONED INDIANA NOODLES

1$^{1}/_{2}$ cups (about) flour

$^{1}/_{2}$ teaspoon salt

$^{1}/_{4}$ teaspoon baking powder

2 large eggs, lightly beaten

1$^{1}/_{2}$ tablespoons (about) milk

Boiling beef broth or chicken broth

COMBINE the flour, salt and baking powder in a large bowl and mix well. Make a well in the center. Drop in the eggs. Mix gently, working in the flour and milk gradually; add additional flour if needed. Divide the dough into halves. Shape each half into a ball on a floured surface. Roll very thin on a floured surface, turning the dough frequently and adding flour as needed; continue to roll out the dough until it becomes thin and pliable. Cut into noodles $^{1}/_{4}$ to $^{1}/_{2}$ inch wide; cut to the desired length. Let dry for about 1 hour. Drop the noodles into the boiling beef broth. Simmer for 15 to 20 minutes or until tender. Serve with braised beef or chicken.

Yield: 4 to 6 servings.

AFTER OPERATING FOR APPROXIMATELY NINETEEN YEARS ON THE SECOND FLOOR OF THE VISITORS CENTER, THE INDIANAPOLIS MUSEUM OF ART-COLUMBUS GALLERY REOPENED IN 1993 IN ITS NEW HOME IN THE COMMONS. IT IS THE ONLY SATELLITE SITE OF THE INDIANAPOLIS MUSEUM OF ART. THIS RELATIONSHIP HAS ALLOWED THE COLUMBUS GALLERY TO HOST MANY EXHIBITS NORMALLY NOT AVAILABLE TO CITIES THE SIZE OF COLUMBUS.

PIEROGIES

1/2 to 1 pound large curd cottage cheese, or shredded farmer's cheese

1 egg, beaten

Pepper to taste

Garlic powder and onion powder to taste

4 cups flour

3 eggs, or 5 egg whites

1 cup water

Boiling water

Butter or margarine

COMBINE the cottage cheese, 1 egg, pepper, garlic powder and onion powder in a medium bowl and mix well. Place the flour in a large bowl. Make a well in the center. Drop in 3 eggs, cutting in with a knife. Add 1 cup water. Knead until a soft dough forms. Divide the dough into halves. Roll each half 1/8 inch thick on a floured board. Cut into circles with a round cutter. Place 1 tablespoon of the cheese mixture on 1/2 of dough circle. Moisten the edge of the dough on that side. Fold the dough over, pressing the edges together firmly to seal. Repeat with the remaining dough and filling. Drop into boiling water in a saucepan. Cook for 5 minutes or until the pierogies float on top of the water. Lift out with a perforated spoon; drain. Place in a serving bowl. Dot with butter. Yield: 32 pierogies.

SIDE DISHES

BREAD AND BUTTER PICKLES

3 cloves of garlic

4 quarts sliced cucumbers (about 16 cups)

6 medium onions, sliced

$1/3$ cup pickling salt

Crushed ice

5 cups sugar

3 cups cider vinegar

2 tablespoons mustard seeds

$1^1/2$ teaspoons ground turmeric

$1^1/2$ teaspoons celery seeds

SPEAR the garlic with wooden picks. Layer the cucumbers, onions, garlic and pickling salt in a large crock or ceramic bowl. Cover with crushed ice. Refrigerate for 3 hours; drain well. Remove and discard the garlic. Combine the sugar, vinegar, mustard seeds, turmeric and celery seeds in a large kettle. Add the cucumbers and onions. Bring to a boil. Pack into hot sterilized pint jars, leaving $1/2$ inch headspace. Prepare the lids using the manufacturer's directions. Wipe the jar rims and adjust the lids on the jars. Process in a boiling water bath for 5 minutes; begin timing when the water returns to a boil. Yield: 8 pints.

DESSERTS

DESSERTS

DESSERTS

CONTENTS

THE FIRST CHRISTIAN CHURCH, 1942, DESIGNED BY ELIEL SAARINEN, TAKEN FROM THE LIBRARY PLAZA WHERE HENRY MOORE'S "LARGE ARCH," 1971, IS THE FOCAL POINT. THE TOWER OF THE BARTHOLOMEW COUNTY COURTHOUSE CAN BE SEEN ABOVE THE TREES IN THE DISTANCE.

APPLESAUCE CAKE WITH BUTTERSCOTCH MERINGUE

2$^1/_2$ cups flour

2 cups sugar

1$^1/_2$ teaspoons baking soda

1$^1/_2$ teaspoons salt

$^1/_4$ teaspoon baking powder

$^3/_4$ teaspoon ground cinnamon

$^1/_2$ teaspoon ground cloves

$^1/_2$ teaspoon ground allspice

1$^1/_2$ cups applesauce

$^1/_2$ cup water

$^1/_2$ cup shortening

2 eggs

1 cup raisins

$^1/_2$ cup chopped walnuts

Butterscotch Meringue

$^1/_2$ cup finely chopped walnuts

BEAT the flour, sugar, baking soda, salt, baking powder, cinnamon, cloves, allspice, applesauce, water, shortening, eggs, raisins and $^1/_2$ cup walnuts in a large mixer bowl at low speed for 30 seconds, scraping the bowl frequently. Beat at high speed for 3 minutes. Spoon into a greased and floured 9x13-inch cake pan. Bake at 350 degrees for 60 to 65 minutes or until a wooden pick inserted near the center comes out clean. Increase oven temperature to 400 degrees. Spread Butterscotch Meringue carefully over the hot cake. Sprinkle with the remaining $^1/_2$ cup walnuts. Bake for 8 minutes or until brown.
Yield: 15 servings.

BUTTERSCOTCH MERINGUE

2 egg whites

1 cup packed brown sugar

1 tablespoon lemon juice

BEAT the egg whites in a mixer bowl until foamy. Add the brown sugar and lemon juice, beating constantly until stiff peaks form.

DESSERTS

CARROT CAKE WITH CREAM CHEESE FROSTING

2 cups flour

1 teaspoon salt

2 teaspoons baking soda

2 teaspoons cinnamon

$1/2$ cup vegetable oil

2 cups sugar

4 eggs

3 cups grated carrots

1 cup chopped pecans

Cream Cheese Frosting

SIFT the flour, salt, baking soda and cinnamon together. Beat the oil and sugar in a mixer bowl. Beat in the eggs. Add the flour mixture gradually, beating well after each addition. Stir in the carrots and pecans. Spoon into 2 greased and floured 9-inch cake pans. Bake at 300 degrees for 30 to 40 minutes or until the layers test done. Cool in the pans for several minutes. Remove to a wire rack to cool completely. Spread Cream Cheese Frosting between the layers and over the top and side of the cake. Yield: 15 servings.

CREAM CHEESE FROSTING

8 ounces cream cheese, softened

$1/4$ cup butter, softened

2 teaspoons vanilla extract

1 (1-pound) package confectioners' sugar

BLEND the cream cheese and butter in a mixer bowl. Add the vanilla and confectioners' sugar, beating until of spreading consistency.

COCOA CAKE WITH CHOCOLATE MARSHMALLOW FROSTING

2 cups sugar

2 cups flour

2 eggs

$^1/_2$ cup margarine

$^1/_2$ cup vegetable oil

$^1/_4$ cup baking cocoa

$^1/_2$ cup buttermilk

1 teaspoon vanilla extract

1 teaspoon baking soda

$^1/_2$ teaspoon salt

Chocolate Marshmallow Frosting

MIX the sugar, flour and eggs in a large bowl. Combine the margarine, oil and cocoa in a saucepan. Heat until the margarine and cocoa melt, stirring occasionally until blended. Pour over the sugar mixture and mix well. Add the buttermilk, vanilla, baking soda and salt and mix well. Spoon into a greased and floured 9x13-inch cake pan. Bake at 400 degrees for 20 minutes. Pour Chocolate Marshmallow Frosting over the hot cake. Yield: 15 servings.

CHOCOLATE MARSHMALLOW FROSTING

$^1/_4$ cup margarine

6 tablespoons evaporated milk

$^1/_4$ cup baking cocoa

$^1/_2$ (1-pound) package confectioners' sugar

$^1/_2$ teaspoon vanilla extract

1 cup chopped pecans

$^1/_2$ cup marshmallows

BRING the margarine, evaporated milk and cocoa to a boil in a saucepan. Remove from the heat. Add the confectioners' sugar, vanilla, pecans and marshmallows, stirring until the marshmallows melt.

DESSERTS

DESSERTS

MRS. FITZGERALD'S GINGERBREAD

This recipe came from architect Edward Charles Bassett.

2 cups flour

1 teaspoon cinnamon

1 teaspoon ginger

1 teaspoon baking soda

$1/8$ teaspoon salt (optional)

1 cup packed light brown sugar

$1/2$ cup butter or margarine, softened

$1/2$ cup light molasses

1 cup hot water

1 egg, beaten

Whipped cream

MIX the flour, cinnamon, ginger, baking soda and salt together. Cream the brown sugar and butter in a mixer bowl until light and fluffy. Add the flour mixture gradually, mixing well after each addition. Add the molasses and water and mix well. Fold in the egg. The batter will be thin. Spoon into a greased 8x8-inch or 9-inch round cake pan. Bake at 350 degrees for 30 minutes or until a wooden pick inserted near the center comes out clean. Top with whipped cream. Yield: 8 to 12 servings.

IN 1981 EDWARD CHARLES BASSETT, PRINCIPAL ARCHITECT WITH SKIDMORE, OWINGS & MERRILL OF SAN FRANCISCO, CALIFORNIA, DESIGNED THE NEW COLUMBUS CITY HALL. THREE STORIES TALL, THE STRIKING 60,000-SQUARE-FOOT STRUCTURE IS A COMMANDING PRESENCE AT THE CORNER OF WASHINGTON AND SECOND STREETS.

HEATH BAR CAKE

$1/2$ cup butter or margarine

2 cups packed dark brown sugar

2 cups flour

1 teaspoon baking soda

1 teaspoon salt

1 cup milk

1 teaspoon vanilla extract

6 frozen Heath bars, crushed

$1/2$ cup chopped pecans

CUT the butter into the brown sugar and flour in a large bowl until crumbly. Remove and reserve 1 cup of the brown sugar mixture. Add the baking soda, salt, milk and vanilla to the remaining brown sugar mixture and mix well; the batter will be very thin. Spoon into a nonstick 9x13-inch cake pan. Sprinkle with a mixture of the reserved brown sugar mixture, candy crumbs and pecans. Bake at 350 degrees for 35 minutes or until the cake tests done. Yield: 12 to 15 servings.

KISS ME CUPCAKES

$2^3/4$ cups flour

$2^1/2$ teaspoons baking powder

1 teaspoon salt

$2/3$ cup margarine, softened

1 cup packed light brown sugar

$3/4$ cup sugar

2 medium eggs

1 teaspoon vanilla extract

$1^1/4$ cups milk

24 chocolate kisses

Confectioners' sugar

MIX the flour, baking powder and salt together. Blend the margarine, brown sugar, sugar, eggs and vanilla in a large mixer bowl. Beat at high speed for 5 minutes, scraping the bowl occasionally. Add the flour mixture and milk alternately, beating well at low speed after each addition. Fill muffin cups $1/3$ full with batter. Top each cupcake with 1 chocolate kiss. Add enough batter to fill muffin cups $2/3$ full. Bake at 350 degrees for 20 to 25 minutes or until the tops spring back when lightly touched. Let cool. Decorate with confectioners' sugar. Yield: 24 servings.

DESSERTS

EASY POUND CAKE

2¹/₄ cups flour

2 cups sugar

¹/₂ teaspoon baking soda

1 teaspoon vanilla extract

1 cup margarine, softened

1 cup lemon yogurt or sour cream

3 eggs

COMBINE the flour, sugar, baking soda, vanilla, margarine, yogurt and eggs in a mixer bowl. Mix at low speed. Beat at medium speed for 3 minutes. Spoon into a greased and floured bundt pan. Bake at 325 degrees for 60 to 65 minutes or until a wooden pick inserted near the center comes out clean. Cool in the pan for 15 minutes. Invert onto a serving plate. Top with favorite glaze or confectioners' sugar. May use nonfat sour cream, egg substitute and plain or vanilla yogurt in this recipe. Yield: 10 servings.

EAT-IT-TOMORROW LEMON CAKE

4 eggs

1 (2-layer) package lemon cake mix

¹/₂ cup vegetable oil

1 package lemon gelatin

1 cup boiling water

Juice of 2 lemons

¹/₂ package lemon confectioners' sugar

BEAT the eggs lightly in a bowl. Add the cake mix, oil, gelatin and water and beat until light. Spoon into a greased and floured 9x13-inch cake pan. Bake at 350 degrees for 20 to 30 minutes or until a wooden pick inserted near the center comes out clean. Pierce several times with a fork. Pour a mixture of the lemon juice and confectioners' sugar over the top. This cake is best served the day after baking. Yield: 15 servings.

SPICE CAKE

2^1/$_2$ cups flour

1 teaspoon baking soda

1 teaspoon baking powder

^{1}/$_2$ teaspoon ground cloves

^{1}/$_2$ teaspoon nutmeg

1 teaspoon cinnamon

^{1}/$_4$ teaspoon salt

^{1}/$_4$ cup mayonnaise-type salad dressing

^{3}/$_4$ cup sugar

2 tablespoons molasses

^{3}/$_4$ cup cold water

SIFT the flour, baking soda, baking powder, cloves, nutmeg, cinnamon and salt together. Mix the salad dressing and sugar in a small bowl. Combine the molasses and water in a large bowl. Add the flour mixture and salad dressing mixture alternately, beating well after each addition. Spoon into 2 greased and floured 9-inch cake pans or a 9x13-inch cake pan. Bake at 350 degrees for 30 to 35 minutes or until the cake tests done. Yield: 10 servings.

FRANKLIN NUT CAKE

3 cups cake flour

1 teaspoon baking powder

1 cup cake flour

2 apples, peeled, chopped

2 bananas, mashed

1 pound pecans or walnuts, chopped

1^1/$_2$ cups butter, softened

2 cups sugar

6 eggs, beaten, or equivalent amount of egg substitute

2 teaspoons vanilla extract

SIFT 3 cups flour with the baking powder. Mix 1 cup flour, apples, bananas and pecans in a bowl. Cream the butter and sugar in a mixer bowl until light and fluffy. Beat in the eggs. Add the baking powder mixture and mix well. Add the fruit mixture and mix well. Stir in the vanilla. Spoon into a greased and floured 10-inch tube pan. Bake at 250 degrees for 3 to 3^1/$_2$ hours or until the cake tests done. Freezes well. Yield: 16 servings.

DESSERTS

BESS'S WHITE CAKE

1 (2-layer) package white cake mix

1 cup milk

$^1/_2$ cup sugar

1 teaspoon almond extract

1 tablespoon cornstarch

Whipped topping

1 cup flaked coconut

PREPARE and bake the cake mix using the package directions for a 9x13-inch glass cake pan. Pierce the cake several times with a fork. Bring the milk, sugar, flavoring and cornstarch to a boil in a saucepan. Boil until thickened, stirring constantly. Pour over the warm cake. Let cool. Top with whipped topping. Sprinkle with the coconut. Chill until serving time. Freezes well. Yield: 15 servings.

BENVENUTI ALMOND COOKIES

$^1/_4$ cup flour

$^3/_4$ cup sugar

2 tablespoons cinnamon

1 tablespoon grated orange peel

$3^1/_2$ ounces almonds, sliced

12 egg whites

$^1/_4$ cup vanilla extract

WIPE a new broom handle clean. Set the broom horizontally across the backs of 2 chairs. Mix the flour, sugar, cinnamon, orange peel and almonds in a bowl. Add the egg whites and vanilla and mix well. Drop by large spoonfuls onto a buttered cookie sheet. Bake at 375 degrees for 8 to 10 minutes or until the edges begin to brown. Remove from the oven. Place the cookies across the broom handle immediately. Hold the cookies on the handle to retain the folded shape until set. May bake up to 6 cookies at once. Rebutter the cookie sheet before each batch.
Yield: $1^1/_2$ to 2 dozen.

ALMOND BRICKLE SUGAR COOKIES

2^1/$_4$ cups flour

1 cup sugar

1 cup butter, softened

1 egg

1 teaspoon baking soda

1 teaspoon vanilla extract

1 (6-ounce) package brickle bits

Sugar

COMBINE the flour, 1 cup sugar, butter, egg, baking soda and vanilla in a large mixer bowl. Beat at medium speed until mixed, scraping the bowl frequently. Stir in the brickle bits. Shape the dough into 1-inch balls. Place 2 inches apart on greased cookie sheets. Flatten to ^{1}/$_4$ inch thick with the bottom of a glass dipped in sugar. Bake at 350 degrees for 8 to 11 minutes or until the edges are light brown. Yield: 4 dozen.

NUT-EDGED BUTTER SLICES

1^1/$_2$ cups flour

2 teaspoons baking powder

^{1}/$_2$ teaspoon salt

^{1}/$_2$ cup butter, softened

^{2}/$_3$ cup sugar

1 egg yolk

2 tablespoons half-and-half

1 teaspoon vanilla extract

1 egg white, lightly beaten

^{1}/$_2$ cup finely chopped pecans

3 tablespoons sugar

SIFT the flour, baking powder and salt together. Cream the butter, ^{2}/$_3$ cup sugar, egg yolk, half-and-half and vanilla in a mixer bowl until light and fluffy. Add the flour mixture gradually, beating well after each addition. Shape into 1^1/$_2$x6-inch rolls. Brush with the egg white. Roll in a mixture of the pecans and 3 tablespoons sugar. Chill until firm. Cut into ^{1}/$_4$-inch slices. Place on a nonstick cookie sheet. Bake at 400 degrees for 6 to 8 minutes or until light brown. Cool on a wire rack. Yield: 3 dozen.

DESSERTS

DESSERTS

COCONUT SNOWBALLS

5 cups sifted flour

1 teaspoon baking soda

2 teaspoons baking powder

$^1/_2$ teaspoon salt

1 cup butter, softened

2 cups sugar

2 eggs

1 teaspoon vanilla extract

$^3/_4$ cup sour cream

1 cup flaked coconut

Tinted sugar

SIFT the flour, baking soda, baking powder and salt together. Cream the butter and sugar in a mixer bowl. Add the eggs and vanilla and mix well. Add the flour mixture gradually, mixing well after each addition. Add the sour cream and coconut and mix well. Chill for several hours. Shape into 1-inch balls. Sprinkle with tinted sugar. Place on a nonstick cookie sheet. Bake at 375 degrees for 10 minutes or until light brown. Yield: 6 dozen.

SIB'S SUPERB CHOCOLATE CHIP COOKIES

4 cups flour

$2^1/_2$ teaspoons baking soda

1 teaspoon salt

$^3/_4$ cup butter, softened

$^3/_4$ cup margarine, softened

$1^1/_4$ cups packed brown sugar

$1^1/_4$ cups sugar

$1^1/_2$ tablespoons vanilla extract

2 eggs

1 to $1^1/_2$ cups lightly toasted chopped pecans

4 cups miniature chocolate chips

MIX the flour, baking soda and salt together. Beat the butter, margarine, brown sugar, sugar, vanilla and eggs in a large mixer bowl until light and fluffy. Add the flour mixture gradually, beating well after each addition. Add the pecans and mix well. Stir in the chocolate chips. Drop by rounded tablespoonfuls 2 inches apart onto a nonstick cookie sheet. Bake at 350 degrees for 10 to 15 minutes or until light brown. Cool slightly on the cookie sheet. Remove to a wire rack to cool completely. Yield: $3^1/_2$ to 4 dozen.

WINTER'S GREAT GINGERSNAPS

These gingersnaps won a Grand Champion ribbon at the county fair.

2 cups flour

2 teaspoons baking soda

1 teaspoon cinnamon

1 teaspoon cloves

1 teaspoon ginger

$^1/_4$ teaspoon salt

$^3/_4$ cup shortening

1 cup sugar

$^1/_4$ cup light molasses

1 egg

Sugar

COMBINE the flour, baking soda, cinnamon, cloves, ginger and salt in a bowl and mix well. Cream the shortening and 1 cup sugar in a mixer bowl until light and fluffy. Add the molasses and egg and beat well. Add the flour mixture gradually, beating well after each addition. Shape into $1^1/_4$-inch balls. Dip in sugar. Place 2 inches apart on a nonstick cookie sheet. Bake at 375 degrees for 10 to 12 minutes or until brown. Yield: 5 dozen.

GOLD COOKIES

$1^1/_2$ cups flour

$^1/_2$ teaspoon baking powder

$^1/_4$ teaspoon salt

$^1/_2$ cup shortening

$1^1/_2$ cups sugar

4 egg yolks

2 tablespoons milk

1 teaspoon vanilla extract

$^3/_4$ cup finely chopped pecans or walnuts

2 teaspoons cinnamon

SIFT the flour, baking powder and salt into a bowl. Cream the shortening, sugar and egg yolks in a mixer bowl until light and fluffy. Stir in the milk and vanilla. Add the flour mixture gradually, beating well after each addition. Chill the dough thoroughly. Shape into small balls. Roll in a mixture of the pecans and cinnamon. Place 3 inches apart on a nonstick cookie sheet. Bake at 400 degrees for 12 to 15 minutes or until golden brown. Yield: 5 dozen.

DESSERTS

DESSERTS

JAM TARTS

1$^1/_2$ cups butter, softened

1 cup sugar

2 egg yolks

1$^1/_2$ teaspoons ground rosemary

1 teaspoon vanilla extract

Grated zest of 1 lemon

3$^3/_4$ cups flour

Jam

Pecan halves

CREAM the butter and sugar in a mixer bowl until light and fluffy. Add the egg yolks, rosemary, vanilla, lemon zest and flour and mix well. Shape into 1-inch balls. Place on a nonstick cookie sheet. Make an indentation in the center of each cookie. Fill with jam. Top with a pecan half. Bake at 325 degrees for 30 minutes or until brown. Yield: 3 to 4 dozen.

LEMON WHIPPERSNAPS

1 (2-layer) package lemon cake mix

1 egg

2 cups whipped topping

1$^1/_2$ cups sifted confectioners' sugar

COMBINE the cake mix, egg and whipped topping in a bowl and mix well. Drop by spoonfuls into the confectioners' sugar. Shape into balls. Place on a greased cookie sheet. Bake at 350 degrees for 10 to 15 minutes or until light brown. Cool on a wire rack. Yield: 2 to 3 dozen.

KOURABIEDES

This recipe came from architect Norman Fletcher.

1¹/₂ cups butter, softened

2 tablespoons confectioners' sugar

1 egg yolk

¹/₂ cup coarsely grated or finely chopped almonds

3¹/₂ cups flour, sifted

2 (1-pound) packages (about) confectioners' sugar

CREAM the butter in a mixer bowl until light and fluffy. Add 2 tablespoons confectioners' sugar and egg yolk and mix well. Beat in the almonds. Add just enough flour gradually to form a soft dough, mixing well after each addition. Shape into 1-inch balls. Place on a nonstick cookie sheet. Bake at 275 degrees for 45 minutes or until very light brown. Cool to lukewarm on the cookie sheet. Sift some of the remaining confectioners' sugar over butcher paper or parchment paper. Transfer the cookies carefully to the butcher paper. Sift confectioners' sugar over the top until the coating is ¹/₄ inch thick or more. Let stand until cool. Yield: 2¹/₂ dozen.

NORMAN FLETCHER, PRINCIPAL ARCHITECT WITH THE ARCHITECTURAL COLLABORATIVE, INC., OF BOSTON, MASSACHUSETTS, DESIGNED THE PARKSIDE ELEMENTARY SCHOOL IN 1962. THE DESIGN OF THIS SCHOOL UTILIZES AN EDUCATION APPROACH EMPHASIZING THE INDIVIDUAL WITHIN HIS OR HER OWN AGE GROUP. IN 1963 FLETCHER DESIGNED THE BARTHOLOMEW CONSOLIDATED SCHOOL CORPORATION ADMINISTRATIVE BUILDING, WHICH SERVES AS CORPORATION HEADQUARTERS. IN 1967 HE DESIGNED THE FOUR SEASONS RETIREMENT CENTER. THERE ARE 91 RESIDENTIAL APARTMENTS IN THIS ONE-LEVEL SENIOR CITIZENS COMPLEX, BUILT ON 25 ACRES OF LANDSCAPED GROUNDS.

DESSERTS

PEANUT BUTTER FUDGE BALLS

2 cups sugar

$^2/_3$ cup milk or 2% milk

1 cup (rounded) peanut butter

1 (7-ounce) jar marshmallow creme

Chopped pecans

COMBINE the sugar and milk in a saucepan, stirring until the sugar dissolves. Bring to a boil. Cook for 4 minutes. Remove from the heat. Add the peanut butter and marshmallow creme and mix well. Pour into a pan to cool. Shape into bite-size balls. Roll in the pecans. Yield: 3 to 4 dozen.

PEANUT BUTTER NO-BAKE COOKIES

2 cups sugar

$^1/_2$ cup baking cocoa

$^1/_4$ cup margarine

$^1/_2$ cup milk

$^1/_2$ cup peanut butter

3 cups rolled oats

$^1/_2$ cup chopped pecans or walnuts

1 tablespoon vanilla extract

BRING the sugar, cocoa, margarine and milk to a boil in a saucepan. Add the peanut butter, oats, pecans and vanilla and mix well. Drop by spoonfuls onto waxed paper. Let stand until hardened. Yield: 4 dozen.

THE "YELLOW NEON CHANDELIER AND PERSIAN WINDOW" BY WORLD-RENOWNED GLASS DESIGNER DALE CHIHULY IS AN EXTRAORDINARY WORK OF ART. THE CHANDELIER IS NINE FEET HIGH AND SIX FEET ACROSS, WEIGHS 12,000 POUNDS, AND IS MADE UP OF 900 PIECES OF HAND-BLOWN GLASS IN FOUR DISTINCT SHAPES AND FOUR SHADES OF YELLOW. THIS WORK DRAMATICALLY HIGHLIGHTS THE TWO-STORY BAY WINDOW AND STAIRCASE OF THE VISITORS CENTER.

SHORTBREAD

Shortbread has always been a tea time favorite and is served with high tea at the Columbus Inn Tea Room.

$1/2$ cup butter, softened

2 tablespoons sugar

$1/4$ cup confectioners' sugar

$1^1/2$ cups flour

Sugar

MIX the butter, 2 tablespoons sugar and confectioners' sugar in a bowl. Add the flour and mix well. Pack into a greased 8-inch round pan; press tightly until well compacted. Prick several times with a fork. Bake at 375 degrees for 30 minutes or until light brown. Sprinkle with sugar. Cut into wedges while hot. Keeps indefinitely. May add $1/4$ cup chopped pecans to the dough for pecan shortbread. Yield: 1 dozen.

COCONUT SHORTBREAD

$1/2$ cup butter, softened

$1/2$ cup shortening

3 tablespoons sugar

2 cups (scant) flour

1 cup flaked coconut

Confectioners' sugar

CREAM the butter, shortening and sugar in a mixer bowl. Add the flour and coconut and mix well. Shape into 2 rolls. Wrap in plastic wrap and chill thoroughly. Cut into slices. Place on a nonstick cookie sheet. Bake at 375 degrees for 15 to 20 minutes or until very light brown. Dip or shake in confectioners' sugar. Do not use margarine in this recipe. Yield: 2 dozen.

DESSERTS

DESSERTS

SNICKERDOODLES

2³/₄ cups flour

2 teaspoons cream of tartar

1 teaspoon baking soda

¹/₂ teaspoon salt

1 cup butter, softened

1¹/₂ cups sugar

2 eggs

1 teaspoon vanilla extract

¹/₄ cup sugar

2 teaspoons cinnamon

SIFT the flour, cream of tartar, baking soda and salt together. Cream the butter and 1¹/₂ cups sugar in a mixer bowl until light and fluffy. Beat in the eggs. Add the vanilla and mix well. Add the flour mixture gradually, beating well after each addition. Chill thoroughly. Shape into balls. Roll in a mixture of ¹/₄ cup sugar and cinnamon. Place on a nonstick cookie sheet. Bake at 400 degrees for 8 to 10 minutes or until light brown; do not overbake. Yield: 2 to 3 dozen.

SUPER SUGAR COOKIES

2¹/₂ cups flour

¹/₄ teaspoon salt

1 cup butter, softened

1 cup sugar

1 egg

1¹/₂ teaspoons grated lemon peel

¹/₂ teaspoon vanilla extract

Tinted canned frosting

MIX the flour and salt together. Cream the butter and sugar in a mixer bowl until light and fluffy. Add egg, lemon peel and vanilla and mix well. Add the flour mixture gradually, mixing well after each addition. Chill overnight. Roll ¹/₄ inch thick on a floured surface. Cut into desired shapes. Place on a nonstick cookie sheet. Bake at 350 degrees for 8 to 9 minutes or until brown. Cool on the cookie sheet for 1 minute. Remove to a wire rack to cool completely. Decorate with frosting. May brush with a mixture of 1 beaten egg white and 2 teaspoons water before baking and sprinkle with tinted sugar; omit the frosting. Yield: 2 to 3 dozen.

WHITE PECAN COOKIES

1 cup butter or margarine, softened

$1/4$ cup sugar

2 teaspoons vanilla extract

2 cups flour

2 cups ground pecans

Confectioners' sugar

CREAM the butter, sugar and vanilla in a mixer bowl until light and fluffy. Add the flour and pecans and mix until crumbly. Shape into small balls. Place on a nonstick cookie sheet. Flatten the cookies, squeezing the edges together if crumbly. Bake at 300 degrees for 40 minutes or until the bottoms are light brown; do not overbake. Roll the warm cookies in confectioners' sugar 4 times or more. Yield: 4 dozen.

FROSTED BANANA BARS

2 cups flour

1 teaspoon baking soda

$1/8$ teaspoon salt

$1/2$ cup butter or margarine, softened

2 cups sugar

3 eggs

$1^1/2$ cups mashed bananas

1 teaspoon vanilla extract

$1/2$ cup butter or margarine, softened

8 ounces cream cheese, softened

4 cups confectioners' sugar

2 teaspoons vanilla extract

MIX the flour, baking soda and salt together. Cream $1/2$ cup butter and sugar in a mixer bowl until light and fluffy. Beat in the eggs, bananas and 1 teaspoon vanilla. Add the dry ingredients and mix well. Spoon into a greased 10x15-inch baking pan. Bake at 350 degrees for 25 minutes or until the layer tests done. Let cool. Cream $1/2$ cup butter and cream cheese in a mixer bowl until light and fluffy. Add the confectioners' sugar and 2 teaspoons vanilla gradually, beating well after each addition. Spread over the baked layer. Cut into bars. Yield: 3 dozen.

DESSERTS

CHERRY CHOCOLATE BARS

1 (2-layer) package chocolate cake mix

1 (21-ounce) can cherry pie filling

2 eggs

1 teaspoon almond extract

1 cup sugar

5 tablespoons margarine

$^1/_3$ cup milk

1 cup semisweet chocolate chips

COMBINE the cake mix, pie filling, eggs and flavoring in a large bowl and mix well. Spoon into a greased and floured 12x15-inch jelly roll pan. Bake at 350 degrees for 20 to 25 minutes or until a wooden pick inserted near the center comes out clean. Cut into bars. Combine the sugar, margarine and milk in a small saucepan. Boil for 1 minute, stirring constantly. Remove from the heat. Stir in the chocolate chips until smooth. Pour over the warm bars. Yield: 3 dozen.

MOTHER'S BROWNIES

$^1/_2$ cup butter or margarine, softened

1 cup sugar

2 eggs

$^2/_3$ cup flour

5 tablespoons baking cocoa

$^1/_2$ teaspoon vanilla extract

$^1/_4$ teaspoon salt

Confectioners' sugar

MIX the butter and sugar in a bowl. Add the eggs and beat until smooth. Add the flour, cocoa, vanilla and salt and mix well. Spoon into a greased 8x8-inch baking pan. Bake at 350 degrees for 20 minutes or until the brownies test done. Dust with confectioners' sugar. Yield: 12 servings.

HOOSIER PEANUT BARS

2 cups flour

1 teaspoon baking soda

1 teaspoon salt

$^1/_2$ cup butter or margarine, softened

$^1/_2$ cup sugar

$^1/_2$ cup packed brown sugar

2 egg yolks

1 teaspoon vanilla extract

2 egg whites

1 cup packed brown sugar

1 cup semisweet chocolate chips

1 cup chopped salted peanuts

COMBINE the flour, baking soda, salt, butter, sugar, $^1/_2$ cup brown sugar, egg yolks and vanilla in a mixer bowl. Blend at low speed until fine particles form. Press into a greased 9x13-inch baking pan. Beat the egg whites in a mixer bowl until foamy. Add 1 cup brown sugar gradually, beating constantly until stiff peaks form. Fold in the chocolate chips and half the peanuts. Spread over the crust. Sprinkle with the remaining peanuts. Bake at 325 degrees for 40 to 45 minutes or until a wooden pick inserted near the center comes out clean; do not overbake. Cut into bars while warm. Yield: 36 servings.

LEMON SPICE DIAMONDS

1 cup flour

1 teaspoon baking powder

$^1/_4$ teaspoon each cinnamon and nutmeg

$^3/_4$ cup shortening

$1^1/_3$ cups packed brown sugar

$^1/_2$ teaspoon vanilla extract

2 eggs

$^1/_2$ teaspoon grated lemon peel

2 tablespoons lemon juice

1 cup rolled oats

$^1/_2$ cup chopped California walnuts

1 cup sifted confectioners' sugar

1 tablespoon lemon juice

Milk

SIFT the first 4 ingredients together. Cream the shortening, brown sugar and vanilla in a mixer bowl until light and fluffy. Beat in the eggs, lemon peel and 2 tablespoons lemon juice. Add the flour mixture gradually, beating well after each addition. Stir in the oats and walnuts. Spread in a greased 9x13-inch baking pan. Bake at 350 degrees for 20 to 25 minutes or until a wooden pick inserted near the center comes out clean. Mix the confectioners' sugar and 1 tablespoon lemon juice in a bowl. Add enough milk to make of a glaze consistency. Pour over the warm dessert. Let cool and cut into diamonds. Yield: 24 servings.

DESSERTS

TERMIGNON AS FRENCH AS APPLE TART

This recipe came from Susan Adams, daughter of architect Bruce Adams.

    1 unbaked pie pastry
    Tart green cooking apples
    Lemon juice or lime juice
    Red currant jelly or other favorite jelly
    Butter

FIT the pie pastry into a quiche pan. Bake at 400 degrees until light brown. Peel and core the apples. Cut into $1/4$- to $1/2$-inch slices. Place the apples in a bowl; sprinkle with lemon juice. Chill for 1 hour or until the apples absorb some of the lemon juice. Arrange in the crust in slightly overlapping concentric circles; the apples should resemble 2 or 3 hoops of overlapping sections. Fill the center with smaller or broken pieces. Melt the jelly and butter in a saucepan, stirring occasionally. Use a pastry brush to paint the apples with the mixture, being careful to cover all the sections. Bake at 325 degrees for 20 to 25 minutes or until the edge of the crust browns. Yield: 6 to 8 servings.

IN 1972 BRUCE ADAMS OF NEW HAVEN, CONNECTICUT, DESIGNED THE PAR 3 GOLF COURSE CLUBHOUSE. PAR 3 IS AN EXCELLENT FACILITY FOR YOUNG GOLFERS LEARNING THE GAME, AND IT IS IDEALLY SUITED FOR LEISURE PLAY AND SENIOR CITIZENS. ADAMS ALSO DESIGNED THE 1973 RENOVATION OF THE COLUMBUS VISITORS CENTER AT FIFTH AND FRANKLIN STREETS IN DOWNTOWN COLUMBUS.

CRANBERRY PIE

1 1/2 cups walnut halves

1 1/2 cups flour

1/4 cup sugar

1 stick butter

1 egg, lightly beaten

1 teaspoon vanilla extract

1/4 cup Triple Sec

1 envelope unflavored gelatin

2 tablespoons sugar

2 tablespoons lemon juice

2 1/4 cups sugar

3/4 cup water

1/2 cup orange juice

1 apple, peeled, shredded

1 pound fresh cranberries

Grated peel of 1 orange

CHOP the walnuts finely in a food processor fitted with a cutting blade. Add the flour and 1/4 cup sugar. Process for several seconds or until mixed. Slice the butter into pats; cut the stick into halves lengthwise. Sprinkle over the walnut mixture. Process until coarse crumbs form. Combine with the egg and vanilla in a bowl, stirring just until moistened. Press onto the bottom and up the side of a lightly greased 10-inch springform pan. Bake at 350 degrees for 18 minutes or until the edge is light brown. Cool in the pan. Mix the Triple Sec, gelatin, 2 tablespoons sugar and lemon juice in a bowl and set aside. Bring 2 1/4 cups sugar, water and orange juice to a boil in a large saucepan, stirring until the sugar dissolves. Boil for 5 minutes. Add the apple. Boil for 1 minute. Add the cranberries. Boil for 5 minutes; the mixture will be almost as thick as jam. Remove from the heat. Stir in the Triple Sec mixture and orange peel. Let cool for 20 minutes, stirring occasionally. Pour over the crust in the pan. Chill for 2 to 3 hours. Serve with whipped cream. Yield: 12 servings.

DESSERTS

BEST-EVER PEANUT BUTTER PIE

3 tablespoons peanut butter

$1/2$ cup confectioners' sugar

$1/2$ cup sugar

3 tablespoons flour

1 tablespoon cornstarch

$1/4$ teaspoon salt

$1^1/2$ cups milk

3 egg yolks, lightly beaten

1 teaspoon vanilla extract

1 baked (8-inch) pie shell

3 egg whites

6 tablespoons sugar

MIX the peanut butter and confectioners' sugar in a bowl until crumbly. Combine $1/2$ cup sugar, flour, cornstarch and salt in a double boiler, mixing with a wooden spoon. Blend in the milk gradually. Add the egg yolks and mix gently. Place over rapidly boiling water so that the double boiler touches the water. Cook for 7 minutes or until thickened and smooth, stirring constantly. Remove from the heat. Add the vanilla, stirring until smooth. Sprinkle all but 2 tablespoons of the peanut butter mixture in the pie shell. Pour the hot filling into the pie shell. Beat the egg whites and 6 tablespoons sugar in a mixer bowl until stiff peaks form. Spread over the filling. Sprinkle with the reserved peanut butter mixture. Bake at 400 degrees until the meringue is golden brown. Filling may be doubled to prepare 2 pies. Yield: 8 servings.

KEY LIME PIE

$1/2$ cup Key lime juice

1 (14-ounce) can low-fat sweetened condensed milk

$1/4$ cup egg substitute

8 ounces light whipped topping

1 (10-inch) graham cracker pie shell

MIX the lime juice, condensed milk and egg substitute in a bowl. Blend in $3/4$ of the whipped topping. Spoon into the pie shell. Chill thoroughly. Use remaining whipped topping to decorate slices. Garnish with a sliver of lime. Yield: 8 to 12 servings.

MOCK PECAN PIE

A blue ribbon winner at the county fair

2 eggs

$^3/_4$ cup sugar

$^1/_2$ cup flaked coconut

$^3/_4$ cup quick-cooking oats

$^3/_4$ cup dark corn syrup

$^1/_4$ cup butter, softened

1 teaspoon vanilla extract

$^1/_8$ teaspoon salt

1 unbaked (8-inch) pie shell

COMBINE the eggs, sugar, coconut, oats, corn syrup, butter, vanilla and salt in a bowl and mix well. Spoon into the pie shell. Bake at 350 degrees for 35 minutes or until the center is set and the crust is brown. Yield: 8 servings.

TRI KAPPA-TAU PECAN PIE

1 (1-pound) package shelled whole pecans or pecan halves

1 unbaked (9-inch) pie shell

2 eggs

2 tablespoons milk

1 cup packed brown sugar

$^1/_2$ cup sugar

1 teaspoon flour

1 teaspoon vanilla extract

$^1/_2$ cup melted butter

ARRANGE the pecans in the pie shell. Mix the eggs, milk, brown sugar, sugar, flour and vanilla in a bowl. Add the butter and mix well. Spoon into the pie shell. Bake at 350 degrees for 50 minutes. Serve with vanilla ice cream. Yield: 6 to 8 servings.

MUCH OF THE CREDIT FOR NURTURING CULTURAL ACTIVITIES GOES TO THE COLUMBUS AREA ARTS COUNCIL, WHICH HAS BEEN OPERATING FOR OVER 25 YEARS. THE COMMUNITY'S INTEREST IN PRESERVING CULTURAL DIVERSITY AND OFFERING AN AMBITIOUS SCHEDULE OF ARTS AND ENTERTAINMENT IS EVIDENT FROM THE CALENDAR OF EVENTS, WHICH INCLUDES SOME 50 ANNUAL FESTIVALS AND EVENTS.

DESSERTS

DESSERTS

RHUBARB CUSTARD PIE

1 packet graham crackers, finely ground

$^1/_4$ cup melted margarine

2 eggs, beaten

2 cups sugar

3 tablespoons flour

$^1/_2$ teaspoon salt

3 cups finely chopped rhubarb

2 tablespoons margarine

$^1/_2$ teaspoon nutmeg

COMBINE the cracker crumbs and $^1/_4$ cup margarine in a bowl and mix well. Press firmly into a 10-inch pie plate. Mix the eggs, sugar, flour and salt in a bowl. Let stand for 15 minutes, stirring twice. Arrange the rhubarb in the pie shell. Pour the egg mixture over the rhubarb. Dot with 2 tablespoons margarine. Sprinkle with the nutmeg. Bake at 400 degrees for 30 minutes. Reduce the oven temperature to 350 degrees. Bake for 30 minutes. May substitute an unbaked pie shell for the graham cracker pie shell. Yield: 8 servings.

STRAWBERRY AND RASPBERRY GLACE PIE

8 ounces cream cheese, softened

2 tablespoons milk

1 baked (9-inch) pie shell

1 pint fresh strawberries

1 pint fresh raspberries

$^3/_4$ cup sugar

2 tablespoons cornstarch

$^1/_3$ cup water

BEAT the cream cheese and milk in a mixer bowl until light and fluffy. Spread $^3/_4$ of the mixture over the bottom and side of the pie shell. Add half the strawberries and raspberries, spreading to cover the bottom of the pie shell. Combine the sugar and cornstarch in a medium saucepan. Add the water and mix well. Add the remaining fruit. Cook until thickened, stirring occasionally. Pour over the fruit in the pie shell. Chill thoroughly. Pipe the remaining cream cheese mixture onto the top of the pie. Yield: 8 to 10 servings.

MARIAN CROUSE'S OLD-FASHIONED SUGAR CREAM PIE

Marian's pies were always the favorite dessert at the First United Methodist Church spring smorgasbord, which raised thousands of dollars for missions. She made six pies each day, and people came early to make sure they got a piece.

1 Old-Fashioned Pie Pastry

1 cup sugar

6 tablespoons flour

1 cup whipping cream

1 cup plus 5 tablespoons half-and-half

1 tablespoon butter

Nutmeg to taste

FIT the pie pastry into a pie plate. Sift the sugar and flour into a bowl. Add the whipping cream, stirring without beating. Add the half-and-half and mix well. Pour into the pie plate. Dot with the butter. Sprinkle with nutmeg. Bake at 450 degrees for 15 minutes. Reduce the oven temperature to 400 degrees. Bake for 45 minutes. Yield: 6 to 8 servings.

OLD-FASHIONED PIE PASTRIES

3 cups flour

1 teaspoon salt

1 cup plus 2 tablespoons shortening

6 tablespoons ice water

MIX the flour and salt in a bowl. Cut in the shortening until crumbly. Stir in the ice water, tossing to mix. Divide into 3 balls. Roll each into a circle on a floured surface.

QUICK-AND-EASY VINEGAR PIE

$1/2$ cup butter, softened

$1^1/2$ cups sugar

2 tablespoons flour

1 tablespoon vanilla extract

2 tablespoons raspberry vinegar

4 eggs, beaten

1 unbaked pie shell

CREAM the butter and sugar in a mixer bowl until light and fluffy. Blend in the flour at low speed. Blend in the vanilla and vinegar. Beat in the eggs at low speed. Spoon into the pie shell. Bake at 300 degrees for 45 minutes or until the center is set. May substitute strawberry, orange or other flavored vinegar for the raspberry vinegar. Yield: 6 to 8 servings.

DESSERTS

DESSERTS

ANNIE'S GREEN TOMATO PIE

This is one of the worst-sounding, but best-tasting, pies ever.

3^1/$_2$ cups quartered green tomatoes, thinly sliced

2 Granny Smith apples, peeled, thinly sliced

^{1}/$_4$ cup raisins

1^1/$_2$ tablespoons vinegar

1^1/$_2$ tablespoons lemon juice

1^1/$_2$ teaspoons salt (optional)

1^1/$_2$ cups sugar

3 tablespoons flour

^{1}/$_8$ teaspoon ground ginger

^{1}/$_2$ teaspoon cinnamon

2 prepared or purchased pie pastries

1 tablespoon fine white bread crumbs

3 tablespoons margarine

COMBINE the green tomatoes, apples, raisins, vinegar, lemon juice and salt in a large bowl and mix well. Mix the sugar, flour, ginger and cinnamon in a small bowl. Fit 1 pie pastry into a 9-inch pie plate. Sprinkle with the bread crumbs. Sprinkle 2 tablespoons of the sugar mixture over the bread crumbs. Add the remaining sugar mixture to the tomato mixture and mix well. Pour into the pie shell and level off. Dot with the margarine. Top with the remaining pastry, sealing the edge and cutting vents. Bake at 425 degrees for 15 minutes. Reduce the oven temperature to 325 degrees. Bake for 50 minutes. Let cool for 2 to 3 hours before serving. Yield: 12 servings.

NEW ORLEANS BREAD PUDDING WITH WHISKEY SAUCE

1 (10-ounce) loaf dried French bread, crumbled

4 cups milk

2 cups sugar

$^1/_2$ cup melted butter

3 eggs, lightly beaten

1 tablespoon nutmeg

2 tablespoons vanilla extract

Whiskey Sauce

COMBINE the bread crumbs, milk, sugar, butter, eggs, nutmeg and vanilla in a bowl and mix well. The mixture should be very moist but not soupy. Pour into a buttered 9x12-inch or larger baking dish. Place in a cold oven. Bake at 350 degrees for $1^1/_4$ hours or until the top is golden brown. Top each serving with Whiskey Sauce. Serve warm. May add 1 cup raisins, 1 cup shredded coconut, 1 cup chopped pecans and/or 1 tablespoon cinnamon to the pudding mixture.
Yield: 15 to 18 servings.

WHISKEY SAUCE

$^1/_2$ cup butter, softened

$1^1/_2$ cups confectioners' sugar

2 egg yolks, beaten

$^1/_2$ cup bourbon, or to taste

CREAM the butter and confectioners' sugar in a saucepan over medium heat. Remove from the heat. Blend in the egg yolks. Add the bourbon gradually, stirring constantly. Let stand until the sauce thickens to the desired consistency.

DESSERTS

CREME AU CHOCOLAT

This recipe came from Susan Girard, wife of architect Alexander Girard.

   3 ounces bittersweet chocolate

   1/4 cup sugar

   3 egg yolks, beaten

   2 teaspoons vanilla extract

   3 egg whites, stiffly beaten

   1 cup slightly sweetened whipped cream

   Grated chocolate

MELT the bittersweet chocolate in a double boiler. Stir in a small amount of water to make a paste. Remove from the heat. Stir in the sugar, egg yolks and vanilla. Fold in the egg whites. Spoon into a serving bowl. Chill for 3 hours to overnight. Top each serving with whipped cream. Sprinkle with grated chocolate. May substitute ground coffee beans for grated chocolate. Yield: 4 servings.

IN 1964 ALEXANDER GIRARD DESIGNED THE WASHINGTON STREET STOREFRONT PLAN, PART OF A BASIC URBAN RENEWAL PLAN STARTED DURING THE 1960'S. GIRARD IS KNOWN FOR HIS DRAMATIC USE OF COLOR.

CHOCOLATE DATE PUDDING

$1/2$ cup sugar

1 tablespoon (rounded) butter

1 cup milk

1 cup flour

2 tablespoons baking powder

1 tablespoon (heaping) baking cocoa

$1/2$ cup chopped dates

$1/2$ cup chopped pecans or walnuts

$1^1/2$ cups packed brown sugar

1 cup hot water

1 tablespoon (rounded) butter

$1/4$ teaspoon salt

1 teaspoon vanilla extract

Whipped topping

MIX the sugar, 1 tablespoon butter, milk, flour, baking powder, cocoa, dates and pecans in a bowl. Combine the brown sugar, water, 1 tablespoon butter, salt and vanilla in a saucepan. Boil for 5 minutes. Pour into an 8x8-inch baking pan. Drop the cocoa mixture by spoonfuls over the brown sugar mixture. Bake at 325 degrees for 45 minutes. Top with whipped topping. Yield: 6 servings.

CRAN-RASPBERRY MOUSSE

1 cup cran-raspberry juice cocktail

1 (3-ounce) package raspberry gelatin

1 (16-ounce) can jellied cranberry sauce

2 cups whipped topping

Frozen raspberries, partially thawed

BRING the juice cocktail to a boil in a saucepan. Remove from the heat. Stir in the gelatin until dissolved. Beat the cranberry sauce at high speed in a mixer bowl for 1 minute. Stir into the gelatin mixture. Chill for $2^1/2$ hours or until thickened. Fold in most of the whipped topping. Spoon into individual dessert dishes. Chill for 3 hours or until firm. Top with the remaining whipped topping and raspberries. Yield: 8 servings.

DESSERTS

DESSERTS

JA CUSTARD

4 cups milk or 2% milk

$^1/_2$ cup sugar or honey

$^1/_4$ teaspoon salt (optional)

4 eggs, beaten, or 8 egg whites, beaten

1 to 2 teaspoons vanilla extract

$^1/_4$ teaspoon nutmeg

BLEND the milk, sugar and salt in a bowl. Add the eggs and beat well. Stir in the vanilla and nutmeg. Pour into a baking dish. Place the baking dish in a pan of water. Bake at 300 to 325 degrees for 1 hour or until a knife inserted near the edge of the baking dish comes out clean. Chill thoroughly. Serve plain or accompanied by coconut rum, grated coconut and chopped or slivered almonds. Yield: 10 servings.

ORANGE RICE PUDDING

1 orange

$^1/_4$ cup sugar

$^1/_4$ cup long grain rice

2 cups milk, scalded

$^1/_8$ teaspoon salt

$^1/_2$ cup half-and-half or light cream

1 egg yolk, lightly beaten

$^1/_4$ cup raisins (optional)

$^1/_4$ teaspoon vanilla extract

PEEL the orange carefully in 1 long unbroken spiral. Reserve the orange for another use. Combine the sugar, rice, milk, orange peel and salt in a double boiler. Cook, covered, over gently boiling water for 45 minutes or until the rice is tender, stirring occasionally during the first part of the cooking time. Remove and discard the orange peel. Mix the half-and-half and egg yolk in a bowl. Stir a small amount of the hot mixture into the egg yolk mixture; stir the egg yolk mixture into the hot mixture. Add the raisins and mix well. Cook, covered, for 45 minutes or until thickened, stirring occasionally. Stir in the vanilla. Serve warm or cool. May top with cinnamon sugar or whipped cream. Yield: 4 servings.

PERSIMMON PUDDING WITH HARD SAUCE OR LEMON SAUCE

1 cup flour

$^3/_4$ cup sugar

$^1/_2$ teaspoon salt

$^1/_2$ teaspoon baking soda

$^3/_4$ cup persimmon pulp

2 eggs, beaten

1 cup milk

1 teaspoon grated lemon peel

2 tablespoons butter, softened

MIX the flour, sugar, salt and baking soda in a bowl. Add the persimmon, eggs, milk, lemon peel and butter and mix well. Spoon into a greased and lightly floured 8x8-inch baking dish. Bake at 350 degrees for 50 minutes or until a knife inserted near the center comes out clean. Serve warm topped with Hard Sauce, Lemon Sauce or whipped cream.
Yield: 6 servings.

HARD SAUCE

$^1/_2$ cup butter, softened

$1^1/_2$ cups sifted confectioners' sugar

2 tablespoons rum or brandy

CREAM the butter and confectioners' sugar in a mixer bowl until light and fluffy. Add the rum and mix well. Chill thoroughly.

LEMON SAUCE

$^1/_2$ cup sugar

2 tablespoons cornstarch

$^1/_8$ teaspoon salt

1 cup boiling water

2 tablespoons butter

Juice of 1 lemon

1 teaspoon grated lemon peel

MIX the sugar, cornstarch and salt in a saucepan. Stir in the boiling water gradually. Cook until thickened, stirring constantly. Remove from the heat. Stir in the butter, lemon juice and lemon peel. Serve warm.

DESSERTS

WHITE HOUSE PUDDING

1 package vanilla wafers, crushed

1 envelope unflavored gelatin

$^1/_4$ cup milk

1 cup sugar

$^3/_4$ cup milk

2 egg yolks

1 teaspoon vanilla extract

2 egg whites, beaten

1 cup nondairy canned milk, beaten

1 can whipped cream (optional)

1 jar maraschino cherries (optional)

LINE a 9x12-inch dish with most of the vanilla wafer crumbs. Soften the gelatin in $^1/_4$ cup milk for 5 minutes. Combine the sugar, $^3/_4$ cup milk, egg yolks and gelatin mixture in a saucepan. Cook until the mixture coats a metal spoon, stirring occasionally. Add the vanilla. Mix the egg whites and nondairy milk in a bowl. Add to the cooked mixture and mix well. Pour into the prepared dish. Chill until firm. Sprinkle with the remaining vanilla wafer crumbs. Cut into squares. Top each serving with whipped cream and a cherry. Yield: 20 servings.

FANTASY FUDGE

3 cups sugar

$^3/_4$ cup butter

1 (5-ounce) can evaporated milk

2 cups semisweet chocolate chips

1 (7-ounce) jar marshmallow creme

1 cup chopped pecans or walnuts

1 teaspoon vanilla extract

COMBINE the sugar, butter and evaporated milk in a saucepan. Bring to a rolling boil. Boil for 5 minutes, stirring constantly. Remove from the heat. Add the chocolate chips, stirring until melted. Add the marshmallow creme, pecans and vanilla and beat well. Pour into a buttered 9x13-inch pan. Let cool. Cut into squares. Yield: 18 to 24 servings.

PEANUT BUTTER WALNUT FUDGE

3 cups sugar

$^3/_4$ cup butter or margarine

$^2/_3$ cup evaporated milk

$^1/_4$ cup (rounded) smooth peanut butter

1 (7-ounce) jar marshmallow creme

1 teaspoon vanilla extract

1 cup (or more) chopped walnuts

COMBINE the sugar, butter and evaporated milk in a heavy medium saucepan. Bring to a rolling boil. Boil over medium heat for 5 minutes, stirring constantly. Remove from the heat. Add the peanut butter, stirring until melted and blended. Add the marshmallow creme, vanilla and walnuts, stirring until mixed. Pour into a greased 9x13-inch pan. Cool to room temperature before cutting into squares. Store in an airtight container in the refrigerator. Pieces will be thin but very rich; for thicker pieces, use a smaller pan. Yield: 18 to 24 servings.

APPLE CRISP

4 cups sliced apples

$^1/_4$ cup water

1 teaspoon cinnamon

1 cup sugar

$^3/_4$ cup flour

$^1/_3$ cup butter, softened

Vanilla ice cream

SPREAD the apples in an 8x8-inch baking pan. Sprinkle with the water and cinnamon. Mix the sugar, flour and butter in a bowl until crumbly. Spread over the apples. Bake at 350 degrees for 40 minutes or until the apples are tender. Top each serving with vanilla ice cream. Yield: 8 to 12 servings.

DESSERTS

BLUEBERRY SOP

This recipe came from Mary Barnes, wife of architect Edward Larrabee Barnes.

> 4 cups wild or cultivated blueberries
>
> 1 cup (scant) sugar
>
> 1 teaspoon cinnamon
>
> $1/2$ cup water
>
> $1/8$ teaspoon salt
>
> Softened butter
>
> 6 slices white bread
>
> Whipping cream

COMBINE the blueberries, sugar, cinnamon, water and salt in a saucepan. Bring to a gentle boil. Cook for 8 to 10 minutes or until the blueberries are tender. Butter the bread generously. Trim off the crusts; cut the bread into strips. Pour about $1/2$ cup of the blueberry mixture into a 1-quart soufflé dish or baking dish. Top with some of the bread strips. Repeat the layers until the dish is full, ending with the blueberry mixture. Chill for 12 hours. Serve with whipping cream or with a dollop of whipped cream. Yield: 8 servings.

IN 1965 EDWARD LARRABEE BARNES OF NEW YORK CITY DESIGNED THE W. D. RICHARDS ELEMENTARY SCHOOL, FEATURING BOLD SLOPING ROOFS FORMING SERRATED SILHOUETTES. EACH ROOM IN A THREE-ROOM CLUSTER HAS ITS OWN OUTSIDE EXIT OPENING ONTO PLAZA AREAS. HE HAS RETURNED TO COLUMBUS TO COMPLETE AN ADDITION TO THIS SCHOOL.

BANANA WALNUT QUESADILLAS

3 tablespoons sugar

$^3/_4$ teaspoon cinnamon

$^1/_8$ teaspoon nutmeg

4 (8-inch) flour tortillas

2 cups coarsely chopped bananas

2 teaspoons lemon juice

$^1/_3$ cup toasted chopped walnuts

1 cup frozen vanilla yogurt

$^1/_4$ cup fat-free caramel topping

MIX the sugar, cinnamon and nutmeg together. Spray 1 side of each tortilla with butter-flavor nonstick cooking spray. Sprinkle coated side with about 1 tablespoon of the sugar mixture. Mix the bananas, lemon juice and remaining sugar mixture in a bowl. Spoon evenly onto the plain side of the tortillas, just slightly off center. Sprinkle with the walnuts. Place a grill rack coated with nonstick cooking spray over medium-hot coals. Grill the tortillas for 30 seconds or until the tortillas are golden brown on the bottom. Fold each tortilla in half. Grill for 30 seconds or until heated through. Spoon the frozen yogurt onto the quesadillas. Drizzle with the caramel topping. Yield: 4 servings.

CHOCOLATE CARAMEL DELIGHT

1 (2-layer) package German chocolate cake mix

1 can sweetened condensed milk

1 jar butterscotch caramel fudge topping

8 ounces whipped topping

Heath bars, crumbled

PREPARE and bake the cake mix using the package directions for a 9x13-inch cake pan. Pierce the warm cake several times with the handle of a wooden spoon. Pour the condensed milk over the cake. Pour the topping over all. Chill, covered, until serving time. Spread with the whipped topping. Sprinkle with the candy.
Yield: 15 to 18 servings.

DESSERTS

CHOCOLATE RASPBERRY TRIFLE

2 packages fat-free vanilla instant pudding mix

1 small jar sugar-free raspberry preserves

1 loaf Entenmann's fat-free chocolate pound cake, sliced

2 (10-ounce) packages frozen raspberries, thawed

8 ounces fat-free whipped topping

PREPARE the pudding mix with skim milk using the package directions. Spread the preserves over the cake slices; cut each slice into cubes. Line an attractive deep bowl with some of the cake cubes. Top with some of the undrained raspberries. Spoon some of the pudding over the top. Repeat the layers until the bowl is full, pressing down each layer. Chill, covered, for 8 hours to overnight. Top with whipped topping just before serving. May use pound cake prepared from Duncan Hines Moist Deluxe devil's food cake mix.

Yield: 8 to 12 servings.

CRANBERRY NESTS

8 sheets phyllo dough

1 cup melted butter

6 tablespoons dry bread crumbs

11 ounces cream cheese, softened

$1/3$ cup confectioners' sugar, softened

Grated zest and juice of 1 lemon

1 (16-ounce) can whole cranberry sauce

1 tablespoon Grand Marnier

$1/2$ cup toasted sliced almonds

BRUSH 1 sheet of dough evenly with butter. Sprinkle with bread crumbs. Repeat the process with 2 more sheets of dough. Top with a plain sheet of dough. Repeat the process for the remaining sheets of dough. Cut into 4-inch squares with a pizza cutter. Fit the squares into lightly buttered muffin cups, leaving the corners pointed up to make "nests." Bake at 350 degrees for 10 to 12 minutes or until golden brown. Whip the cream cheese, confectioners' sugar, lemon zest and lemon juice in a bowl. Blend the cranberry sauce and Grand Marnier in a bowl. Fill the "nests" $1/3$ full with cream cheese filling. Spoon 2 to 3 teaspoons of the cranberry mixture into each nest. Top with almonds.

Yield: 24 servings.

CREAM PUFFS WITH VANILLA FILLING AND CHOCOLATE GLAZE

1 cup water

6 tablespoons butter or margarine

1 cup flour

4 eggs

Vanilla Filling

Chocolate Glaze

BRING the water and butter to a boil in a saucepan over medium heat. Remove from the heat. Add the flour all at once, stirring vigorously with a wooden spoon. Cook for 1 minute, stirring constantly. Pour into a large bowl. Beat in the eggs 1 at a time. Drop by slightly rounded tablespoonfuls onto a baking sheet. Bake at 425 degrees for 20 to 25 minutes or until golden brown. Remove from the oven. Cut a 1-inch horizontal slit in the side of each puff. Turn off the oven. Let the puffs stand in the oven for 5 minutes or until dry on the inside. Cut the puffs into halves at the slit. Fill each puff with 2 to 3 tablespoons Vanilla Filling. Top with Chocolate Glaze. Replace the cream puff tops. Yield: 10 to 15 servings.

VANILLA FILLING

2 cups whipping cream

1 (4-ounce) package French vanilla instant pudding mix

BEAT the whipping cream and pudding mix in a mixer bowl for $1^1/_2$ to 2 minutes or until smooth. Chill for 10 minutes or longer. May substitute chocolate pudding mix for the French vanilla.

CHOCOLATE GLAZE

$^3/_4$ cup semisweet chocolate chips

$1^1/_2$ tablespoons butter or margarine

$1^1/_2$ teaspoons light corn syrup

COMBINE the chocolate chips, butter and corn syrup in a microwave-safe bowl. Microwave until the chocolate and butter melt. Cool to room temperature.

DESSERTS

DESSERTS

EASY CRUMB CAKE

$3/4$ cup margarine, softened

$1/4$ cup sugar

$1^1/2$ cups flour

1 egg

1 teaspoon vanilla extract

2 cans pie-sliced apples

$3/4$ cup margarine, softened

$1/2$ cup sugar

$1^1/2$ cups flour

$1/2$ teaspoon cinnamon

Confectioners' sugar (optional)

MIX $3/4$ cup margarine, $1/4$ cup sugar, $1^1/2$ cups flour, egg and vanilla in a bowl. Pat onto the bottom and up the sides of a 10x15-inch baking pan. Arrange the apple slices in the pan. Mix $3/4$ cup margarine, $1/2$ cup sugar, $1^1/2$ cups flour and cinnamon in a bowl until crumbly. Sprinkle over the apples. Bake at 350 degrees for 1 hour or until light brown. Sprinkle with confectioners' sugar. May substitute cherry or blueberry pie filling for the apples. Yield: 15 servings.

FIESTA FINALE

2 cups chopped hulled strawberries

2 kiwifruit, peeled, chopped

1 can mandarin oranges, drained

$1/3$ cup sugar

1 teaspoon ground cinnamon

12 (7- to 9-inch) flour tortillas

8 ounces Neufchâtel cheese, softened

$1/2$ cup orange juice

3 tablespoons honey

COMBINE the strawberries, kiwifruit and oranges in a bowl and mix well. Chill, covered, for up to 4 hours. Mix the sugar and cinnamon in a small bowl. Cut each tortilla into 6 equal wedges. Dip each wedge lightly into water, then into the sugar mixture. Arrange in a single layer on an oiled baking sheet. Bake at 500 degrees for 3 to 4 minutes or until crisp and golden brown. Cool on a wire rack. Combine the cheese, orange juice and honey in a 2-quart saucepan. Cook over low heat for 3 minutes, whisking constantly. Mound the warm tortilla pieces on a dessert platter. Serve the cheese sauce and fruit salsa on the side. Yield: 30 servings.

LEMON ANGEL SQUARES

1 package lemon gelatin

1 (6-ounce) can frozen lemonade concentrate, thawed

3 cups whipped topping

1 large angel food cake, torn into 1-inch pieces

$^1/_2$ cup flaked coconut

Whipped topping

PREPARE the gelatin using the package directions. Chill until partially set. Add enough water to the lemonade concentrate to measure 2 cups. Stir into the gelatin. Whip until foamy. Stir in 3 cups whipped topping. Add the cake pieces and mix well. Pour into a greased 9x13-inch pan. Sprinkle with the coconut. Chill for 4 hours to overnight. Cut into squares. Serve with additional whipped topping. Yield: 8 to 10 servings.

MYSTERY TORTE

3 egg whites

$^1/_2$ teaspoon baking powder

1 cup sugar

$^2/_3$ cup chopped walnuts or pecans

16 butter crackers, crushed

1 teaspoon vanilla extract

1 cup whipping cream, whipped, or 1 cup whipped topping

Chopped walnuts or pecans

BEAT the egg whites in a mixer bowl until foamy. Add the baking powder and sugar gradually, beating constantly until stiff peaks form. Add the walnuts, cracker crumbs and vanilla and mix well. Spoon into a lightly buttered 8-inch pie plate. Bake at 350 degrees for 30 minutes. Let cool. Top with the whipped cream. Garnish with additional walnuts. Chill for 3 hours or longer.
Yield: 6 servings.

DESSERTS

DESSERTS

PEANUT BUTTER CHOCOLATE CHEESECAKE

1 1/4 cups chocolate graham cracker crumbs

1/2 cup chopped peanuts

1/4 cup sugar

1/3 cup melted margarine

1 cup sugar

1/4 cup packed brown sugar

24 ounces cream cheese, softened

1 3/4 cups chunky peanut butter

2 eggs

2/3 cup evaporated milk

2 tablespoons cornstarch

1 teaspoon margarine

1 ounce unsweetened chocolate

1/4 cup confectioners' sugar

1 teaspoon dark corn syrup

2 teaspoons boiling water

1/2 teaspoon vanilla extract

Miniature peanut butter cups

COMBINE the cracker crumbs, peanuts, 1/4 cup sugar and 1/3 cup margarine in a bowl and mix well. Press over the bottom and 1 inch up the side of a 9-inch springform pan. Bake at 350 degrees for 6 to 8 minutes or until light brown. Cream 1 cup sugar, brown sugar and cream cheese in a mixer bowl until light and fluffy. Beat in the peanut butter, eggs and evaporated milk. Add the cornstarch and beat well. Pour into the crust. Bake at 350 degrees for 55 to 60 minutes or until the edge is set and the center moves slightly. Cool completely on a wire rack. Chill thoroughly. Combine 1 teaspoon margarine, chocolate, confectioners' sugar, corn syrup and boiling water in a saucepan. Cook over low heat until the chocolate melts, stirring frequently. Stir in the vanilla. Pour over the cheesecake. Chill for 3 hours before serving. Decorate with miniature peanut butter cups. May top with chopped peanuts, chocolate chips and/or peanut butter chips. Yield: 12 to 16 servings.

FRESH PEACH COBBLER

This recipe came from Sue Paris, wife of architect Jim Paris.

6 (or more) large peaches

$^1/_2$ cup sugar

1 cup flour

$^1/_8$ teaspoon salt

1 teaspoon baking powder

1 cup sugar

1 egg

$^1/_2$ cup melted butter or margarine

$^1/_2$ teaspoon vanilla extract

SLICE the peaches into a buttered 7x11-inch baking dish. Add $^1/_2$ cup sugar and mix well. Combine the flour, salt, baking powder, 1 cup sugar, egg, butter and vanilla in a bowl and mix well. Spoon into the baking dish. Bake at 350 degrees for 30 minutes or until golden brown. Yield: 6 servings.

JIM PARIS OF COLUMBUS, INDIANA, DESIGNED THE IVY TECH STATE COLLEGE BUILDING AND THE ADDITIONS AND RENOVATIONS TO FIRE STATION NO. 1, CLEO ROGERS MEMORIAL LIBRARY, AND THE SENIOR CENTER.

DESSERTS

DESSERTS

CINNAMON NUTS

This recipe came from architect Robert Trent Jones.

  1 cup sugar

  $1/4$ teaspoon salt

  $1/2$ teaspoon cinnamon

  6 tablespoons milk

  $1^1/2$ to 2 cups pecan or walnut pieces

  $1/2$ teaspoon vanilla extract

COMBINE the sugar, salt, cinnamon and milk in a saucepan. Bring to a boil. Cook to 238 degrees on a candy thermometer, soft-ball stage, stirring frequently. Remove from the heat. Add the pecans and vanilla. Turn the mixture over and over with a spoon until the pecans are thoroughly covered and the mixture has begun to sugar. Turn onto waxed paper. Separate into clusters.

Yield: 15 to 18 servings.

IN 1964 ROBERT TRENT JONES OF MONTCLAIR, NEW JERSEY, DESIGNED OTTER CREEK GOLF COURSE. LOCATED JUST EAST OF COLUMBUS, 380 ACRES OF HILLY TERRAIN AND THOUSANDS OF TREES ARE A NATURAL SETTING FOR THE MAGNIFICENT DESIGN. OTTER CREEK, A PUBLIC GOLF COURSE ALWAYS IN TOURNAMENT CONDITION, HAS BEEN RATED IN THE TOP 25 PUBLIC COURSES IN THE UNITED STATES SINCE ITS INCEPTION IN 1964. JONES RETURNED TO OTTER CREEK IN 1982 TO UPDATE HIS DESIGN SO THAT THE COURSE REMAINS A SERIOUS TEST OF GOLF, ABLE TO MATCH TODAY'S NEW CLUB AND BALL TECHNOLOGY.

BIBLIOGRAPHY

A LOOK AT ARCHITECTURE—COLUMBUS, INDIANA, 1991, Columbus Visitors Center, Columbus, Indiana.

Columbus, Indiana: People and Their Buildings, video by Dan Cornish, Cornish Productions.

Columbus, Indiana: People and Their Buildings, an exhibit designed by Tony Spagnola, Spagnola and Associates.

CONSTRUCTION DIGEST, March 11, 1996, page 11.

HISTORY OF BARTHOLOMEW COUNTY, INDIANA—1888. An annotated edition of the Bartholomew County Section of the 1888 Bartholomew County History, including biographies, with addition of new editor's notes, addenda articles, old photographs and maps, volume one, Robert J. Marshall, Miss Mildred Murray and Ross G. Crump, editors.

Internet, Freshmen, 4, web site page, April 4, 1997.

Map and Tour Guide for Historical Columbus, Indiana, Preserve to Enjoy, 1991.

NATIONAL GEOGRAPHIC, volume 154, number 3, September 1978, page 390.

1997 COLUMBUS INDIANA VISITORS GUIDE, Published by Indiana Business Magazine, Custom Publishing, 1997.

STAMBERG AFERIAT ARCHITECTURE, Rizzoli International Publications, 1997.

THE GOAL POST, U.S. Postal Service, Indianapolis MSC Employees Newsletter, volume one, number one, page seven.

INDEX

INDEX

ORDER INFORMATION

Visitors Center, Inc.
506 Fifth Street
Columbus, Indiana 47201
800-468-6564 • 812-378-2622
email: visitcol@hsonline.net

Please send _____ copies of SIMPLY THE BEST . . . RECIPES BY DESIGN $18.95 each $ _____

Plus shipping $4.00 each $ _____

Indiana residents add   5% sales tax $ _____

TOTAL $ _____

Name _____

Address _____

City/State/Zip _____

Telephone Number _____

Method of Payment: ☐ Check or Money Order   ☐ VISA   ☐ MasterCard

Card Number _____   Expiration Date _____

Signature _____

Make checks payable to Visitors Center, Inc.

This page may be photocopied.

VISITORS CENTER, INC.

506 Fifth Street

Columbus, Indiana 47201

800-468-6564

812-378-2622

http://www.columbus.in.us

e-mail: visitcol@hsonline.net